PUNKS ON SCOOTERS
THE BRISTOL MOD REVIVAL 1979-1985

MICHAEL W SALTER

THIS BOOK IS DEDICATED TO THE MEMORY OF NEIL (BABY) GARLAND WHO EMBRACED THE SCOOTER SCENE WITH AN ENTHUSIASM AND JOY THAT ONLY YOUTH CAN BRING.

BRISTOL ARCHIVE RECORDS

Punks on Scooters
The Bristol Mod Revival 1979-1985
By Michael W Salter
First published September 2016 by Tangent Books &
Bristol Archive Records. Reprinted October 2016.

Tangent Books
Unit 5.16 Paintworks
Bristol
BS4 3EH
0117 972 0645
www.tangentbooks.co.uk
Email: richard@tangentbooks.co.uk

ISBN 978-1-910089-44-6

Design & Illustrations: Nicholas Darby

Copyright: Michael W Salter/Tangent Books/
Bristol Archive Records

Copyright of the photographs pages 124-127 rests with the original photographers and we thank them for their contribution.

Michael W Salter has asserted his right under the Copyright, Designs and Patents Act of 1988 to be identified as the author of this work. This book may not be reproduced or transmitted in any form or by any means without the prior written consent of the publisher, except by a reviewer who wishes to quote brief passages in connection with a review written in a newspaper or magazine or broadcast on television, radio or on the internet.

A CIP record of this book is available at the British Library.

Printed in the UK using paper from a sustainable source.

WITH SPECIAL THANKS TO THIS MOTLEY BUNCH, WITHOUT WHOM NONE OF THIS WOULD HAVE HAPPENED... 2 Tone, Andrew 'Foxy' Faulks, Adrian Sutton, Alex Briggs, Alison Dixon, Alison White, Andrew Ashman, Andrew Baker, Andrew Harvey, Andrew Selwood, Andy Bendall, Andy Britton, Andy Nethercott, Andy Smith, Angelo LaBruno, Barbara Salter, Brad Veale, Carole Tsang, Caroline Humphries, Catherine Beedle, Charles Philips, Chiara, Chris Pugh, Chris Stretch, Claire Belcher, Cockney Ken, Cockney Simon, Colin Musty, Conway, Craig Dyer, Craig Lester, Dale Brice, Daniel Diorazio, Danny Milkins, Darren Pullman, Darron Hacker, Daryl Hicks, Dave Cox, Dave Hall, Dawn Parfitt, Daygan Robinson, Dean Read, Dean Strange, Debbie Stabbins, Debbie Yeomans, Denbigh Mudge, Dennis Lane, Derek Lyons, Colin Luft, Dexter Perry, Doug Poole, Elaine Howard, Elaine Lempsink, Elly Horne, Eve Pearce, Fiona Poole, Fred, Gary Peck, Gary Thomas, Geoff Rice, Geoff Taylor, Geoff Twitchen, Geraldine Allen, Gerry McCabe, Giuseppe 'Joe' Graffagnino, Gordon Tiley, Grant Williams, Mike Thomas, Greg Embury, Helen Whittle, Ian Green, Ian Williams, Jane Marren, Jane V, Jem Wade, Jenny Lee, Jer Crew, Jerry Cripps, Jim Baker, Jock, Joe Elmer James, Joe Staples, John 'Locomotion' Andrews, John Ballentyne, John Britton, John Dicker, John Hooker, John Wherlock, Karen Ashford, Kelvin Blake, Kelvin Harvey, Kev Jarvis, Kev Lucas, Kev Norton, Kira Blake, Lee Collins, Leon Phipps, Les Gilson, Lewis, Liz Gaynard, Mad Sue, Lin Henley, Malcolm Beedle, Mark DeBarton, Mark O'Neil, Martin Hamm, Martin White, Martyn Rogers, Michael Furzeman, Mike Darby, Mike Hooper, Mike Jakes, Mitch Smith, Mitch Wilson, Neil Garland, Neil Grimstead, Neil Hynam, Neil Oliver, Neil Whitfield, Neil Wicks, Nicci Powell, Nick Rippington, Nina Martin, Nuala Minty, Paddy Smith, Pat Evans, Patrick Morgan, Paul 'Toby' Salter, Paul Hannam, Paul McCarthy, Paul Rogers, Paul Slaney, Paul Wooten, Pete Nethercott, Phil Hamm, Phil Riley, Philip Henley, Piggy, Rich Brown, Rich Pinaccia, Richard Denning, Rob Merrill, Rob Wollacott, Ron Wickens, Rosemary Smith, Ross Kirby, Sally Twitchen, Sally Ronchetti, Samantha Messer, Sarah Boniface, Scumbag, Sean Parry, Sharon Bentley, Simon Phillpotts, Simon Turner, Skip Hawker, Steffan Block, Steve Bush, Steve Dixon, Steve Everitt, Steve Jones, Steve Lewis, Steve Mathews, Stuart Lanning, Sue Allen, Sue Hunt, Terri Bright, Tim Bond, Tim Bryer, Tim Coles, Tim Hooper, Tim McGill, Tina Nawrocki, Toby Brown, Tom Bennett, Tom Russell, Tony Mills, Vince Ayres, Wayne Belcher.

A very special thank you to all the people that have put aside their valuable time to help with the writing of this book. Also the many friends and family that have been not only supportive, but also incredibly resilient having listened to many of the stories contained herein, over and over again during the last two years, your faith in this project has been more than appreciated. And finally to all those that were not mentioned within these pages, be assured you are part of them.

INTRODUCTION

C1 **BORED TEENAGERS** 19

C2 **THE MOD REVIVAL** 37

C3 **THE CALL OF CARNABY STREET** 46

C4 **THE LOCARNO AND SUBURBAN VIOLENCE** 61

C5 **SCOOTERS AT THE JOLLY COBBLER** 84

C6 **ON THE ROAD** 89

C7 **LOCARNO TO RAQUEL'S TO STEAMERS** 103

C8 **RETURN OF THE SCOOTER BOY** 117

APPENDICES 141

Eve Pearce
Geoff Rice
Jon Andrews
Jerry Cripps
The Newbeats and Colonel Kilgore's

INTRODUCTION

When I was asked to work on a new project by Bristol Archive Records and Tangent Books, about what was probably the happiest time of my life, I jumped at the chance because a chronicling of these events seemed long overdue.

Admittedly, the first thought that sprang to mind was the old adage 'if you can remember it, you weren't there'. I had proof of this in my working life when Mike D'Abo, he of Manfred Mann fame, was presenting a radio show I was working on. Regaling the audience with insider titbits and stories of his high times during the 1960s, he seemed to either have forgotten about what was probably the highlight of his musical career, or was blatantly making it up as he went along. When I asked him after the show about his rather dubious recollection of facts, he turned to me with a wry smile and simply said, "Mike, I was there."

I don't pretend to remember everything that went on during the years covered by this book. But with the help of a few friends, I've tried to tell the story of what it was like for us to grow up in Bristol, England between 1979 and 1985, with punk and then the mod revival as a soundtrack to our lives.

What isn't tolerated today could be quite common place in the late 1970s to mid eighties. This was a time of ageing teddy boys, motor cycle gangs, punks, rude boys, skinheads, rockabillies, heavy metal kids, disco types called kitters and of course mods, all vying for some sort of supremacy on the streets and on the dance floor.

Being part of a scene or tribe was exciting but these were also violent times on the streets of Bristol. It's too easy to blame the violence entirely on the tribes, but we were growing up in a time of major economic and political upheaval. We felt ignored and disenfranchised.

The British population was getting disenchanted with the Labour government which came to power in 1974. Prime Minister Harold Wilson had stepped down after two years, handing the Premiership over to Jim Callaghan, who was to lead his party disastrously until December 1979 when Callaghan was famously defeated in the General Election, by greengrocers' daughter Margaret Thatcher.

By the tail end of 1979 there was a sense of decline in the air; Britain was in the 'winter of discontent'. A discontent perpetuated by four years of pay restraints implemented by the Labour government, after the humiliation of being the first Western country to borrow money from the International Monetary Fund, money loaned on the condition that the British government would have to make very deep cuts in its spending.

After four years the Trade Unions had had enough. They were no longer prepared to endure continuing economic hardship and resorted to industrial action. The petrol tanker and lorry drivers were first to strike, soon followed by hospital ancillary staff, ambulance drivers and dustbin collectors. Hospitals were picketed, the dead left unburied. Eventually it got so bad the army were called in to deal with the thousands of rats swarming around the heaps of uncollected, rotting, acrid rubbish. Britain as I remember it was in a terrible state both politically and culturally.

The large number of simultaneous strikes and the general undercurrent of violence created a sense of alarm in the population about the decline of British society.

There seemed to be violence of some sort everywhere, if it wasn't on your doorstep, then all you had to do was turn on the TV set (preferably the BBC as ITV had gone off air for several months due to strikes) and you could catch up with such gruesome reports as the Yorkshire Ripper's latest God-guided exploits, as he brutally murdered with what seemed complete impunity, at least 13 prostitutes as far afield as Yorkshire and Greater Manchester.

The media daily reported incidences of rape, knife crime, vandalism and assault. No one seemed safe. Even the police had almost thrown in the towel admitting they were at a loss to what the solution may be, whilst trying to accrue public support and sympathy by citing poor staffing levels and promising to 'get back to community policing' rather than whizzing around in their Panda Cars thinking they were TV cops Regan and Carter from *The Sweeney*.

If you were able to avoid all this media doom and

gloom about crime, the state of the economy and rising unemployment, which was to top three million, then it was almost impossible to miss the politically motivated graffiti daubed across the many, bridges, walls and filthy urine-smelling bus shelters on the streets of Britain.

These non-stylistic statements, unlike the commissioned artwork of today, would usually promote words of limited wisdom from such factions as the IRA or the National Front, hoping to swell support and garner some sympathy for their causes.

It was inevitable that British youth felt a need to express its anger and frustration at what seemed to be 'futureless politics'. It was an anger and frustration that had found a youthful voice with the emergence of punk rock, bringing with it a huge explosion of politics in music, with such songs as 'Anarchy in the UK' 'God Save the Queen' and later on 'Eton Rifles,' distinguishing punk as an overtly politicised youth culture.

Many of the leading punk and reggae bands played a major role in the Rock Against Racism movement. This was a campaign set up to discourage young people from embracing racism, after an increase in racial conflict, partly perpetuated by the economic climate; a climate that helped fuel the unsettling growth of white nationalist groups such as the British Movement and the more popular National Front.

By 1979 the National Front were at the peak of

their powers. Supported by a hard core of neo-Nazi skinheads they had grown through the 1970s to become a worrying political force in England, fielding just over 300 candidates and polling nearly 200,000 votes in the 1979 General Election. Many of the skinheads were white supremacists, opposed to non-white immigration and committed to a programme of repatriation, which in less subtle words meant 'blacks go home'.

These skinheads were unlike the original 1960s skinheads that grew out of a split between the fashion conscious mods and their more violent working class counterparts around 1966. Known as hard mods, gang mods, lemonheads or peanuts they were identified by their shorter hair and more working class image. These hard mods became commonly known as skinheads sometime around 1968. In addition to retaining many mod influences, early skinheads were very interested in Jamaican rude boy styles and culture, especially the music: ska, rocksteady, and early reggae, with hardly a hint of racism.

Ironically this new breed of skinhead, although racist, besides having their own bands like Cock Sparrer and Sham 69 were also drawn towards the same black-rooted music as their predecessors. Many gigs I attended were often disrupted by the Skinheads chanting 'Sieg Hiel' accompanied by the Nazi salute, usually followed by various levels of violence breaking out either in the crowd or aimed at the bands. It wasn't uncommon to see a hail of beer glasses smashing around those on stage, especially any with mixed-race line ups such as The Specials and The Selecter.

Pauline Black of The Selecter said:

'You've got to remember that there were six black people in the original band and one white person, so we were easily targetable. We used to be known in those days The Selecter plus six, and The Specials because they had two black members in their band were known as The Specials plus two. That was the kind of division that there was.'

Pauline recalled a particular Selecter concert in Bristol...

'As soon as we went on stage, pretty much after the first song everyone just sort of began this huge ruck. The guy who was promoting the gig, he and another bouncer they waded in. They had this wonderful technique. They would walk up to a trouble maker and sink their teeth into the person's ear lobe and that would be it, and then they would be carried out because if you have ever had someone sink their teeth into your ear it's either your ear comes off or you go quietly... but that was definitely between mods and skinheads.'

The skinheads as far as I remember were the most feared of all the sub cultures. They seemed quite happy to fight anyone including their own for little or no reason. Many skinheads had become accomplished at 'gang warfare' learning their fighting skills and tactics in the side streets or on the football terraces up and down the country,

INTRODUCTION

during what has become known as the Golden Age of Hooliganism. And to top it all police were at a loss as what to do about it.

Britain, for some, was a thoroughly depressing place. That is unless you were a teenager with a sense of adventure...

Chapter 1

BORED TEENAGERS

In 1976 I was convinced I could get into the sixth form of The Ridings High School in Winterbourne Bristol. I'd been there for five years and enjoyed every moment of it. To be honest, I had never actually considered that one day I would have to leave and get a job. After all, what harm would another 12 months do?

I still remember being called in for the interview, which I assumed was just a formality as surely the school was in need of another year of my class antics and disruptions? This ill-conceived plan of mine was to come to an abrupt halt, when the head of the sixth form, Mr Lines, said, "Well Michael, you haven't managed to learn anything in the five years you have been here. I doubt very much that you will learn anything in another. Close the door on your way out."

Now this all came as something of a shock as I'd never really expected to be leaving what was in effect my second home. School was my playground and the thought of moving on wasn't something I had prepared for.

I went to see Miss Stansell the careers officer, a small, quite officious woman who only seemed to appear just before the mass exodus of graduating pupils entered the brave new world of work and bills. I can't say I remember too much of our brief meeting, but I do recall her asking... 'Now Michael what is it you would like to do when you leave?' I pondered for a moment, because I hadn't given it too much thought in the five joyous years I had spent as the class clown. For some reason I had a flash of inspiration when a vision of a very high Madison Ave office block came to mind, with me suitably tailored, looking out from my expensively furbished office across the sprawling New York skyline...

"I quite see myself as an advertising executive," I confidently replied.

Calculatingly she picked up a large folder from her desk and pulled out a small piece of paper, after pausing for a few moments she removed her glasses and stared almost sympathetically at me.

"Well," she said "After looking at your exam results, have you ever considered being a milkman? That involves selling things and meeting people."

I stood for what seemed an eternity, feeling completely deflated as the reality of my situation slowly sank in, I closed the door on the way out.

Weighing up my options between getting up at 4am or staying in bed, I decided to go and work for the Government or Moss Bros as we called it, the Ministry of Social Security... I signed on the dole.

In those days the nice people at the dole office seemed only too happy to hand over £12 a fortnight to an academic failure such as I. As long as I could sign on the dotted line, they would leave me to my own devices for another couple of weeks; £5 to mum, £4 to me, to spend on lager and cigarettes.

The rest I would just waste.

   Eventually it was made very clear that it was time I should venture out into the great wide world and get myself a paying job; not only by the ever-patient people at the dole office but also my irascible step father. He was becoming rather irritated by the fact that I was still in bed when he went off to work in the morning, and more than likely still there when he returned home each evening. Getting a job seemed completely at odds with the rather nice social lifestyle I had managed to carve out for myself around the public houses of Winterbourne and Frampton Cotterell over the previous six months.

   The first time I'd managed to get served alcohol was at the grand age of 16 in The Globe public house, just around the corner from where I lived. Being two years shy of the legal age limit and certainly not looking 18, I was obviously quite nervous about the whole thing. Not only was I worried about being refused service, but also having to walk into the pub on my own. As I opened the Globe's front door with a fair amount of trepidation, I was greeted by a rather high-pitched voice from behind the bar... 'fuck off' came the surprisingly unfriendly greeting, I stood there mortified assuming I'd been sussed well before I'd even got into the pub. 'Go on fuck off' came the voice once again, as if the first greeting wasn't enough. Crest fallen I abruptly turned on my heels, only to hear a rather ear-piercing squawk, quickly followed by what I can only describe as a very loud farting noise, as I glanced over my shoulder I noticed to my utter relief a very content looking, myna bird swinging happily backwards and forwards on its perch reciting a foul-mouthed repertoire taught to him by the pub's regulars.

Drinking has always been part and parcel of growing up for many, in fact without it many of the stories in this book would never have happened. Some can take it or leave it whereas others can make a career out of it; I was very quickly falling into the latter category. My first real experience of alcohol had come during the wonderful carefree summer of 1976 when I was invited to visit my long-absent but much-loved alcoholic father at his new address in Chelmsford, Essex where he had become the proud owner of the Three Horseshoes public house, and yes you did read that right my alcoholic father had now become the custodian of his own unlimited supply of alcohol.

At a loss to know what to do with me for two weeks I was regularly driven at great speed through the country lanes of Essex by my very drunk and long-banned-from-driving father to anywhere he thought might keep me engaged, which usually meant one of the many watering holes as he called them dotted around the Chelmsford area. To be honest I really enjoyed the thrill of those death-defying drives that is until he explained that the scar that went from one side of his neck to the other was a proud memento from an earlier time when he had been catapulted head first through the car window and almost decapitated himself. Dad obviously had his own demons which I assume he had tried to keep at bay by placating them with as much alcohol as they requested; dad was very strong on customer service.

Within the year dad was dead. He tried to shoot his new wife with a rifle that was purportedly just lying around the premises, from that point on everything very quickly went downhill. After his arrest he was sent to Chelmsford prison where he was treated for depression while the Crown compiled charges of attempted murder and possession of a firearm. Once on bail he bought himself a nice new car drove it into his recently deceased mother's garage, and with his best friend (a bottle of whiskey) to keep him company he slowly drifted off, hopefully to some eternal peace of mind. He was only 39.

Back in Frampton, day after day I was reminded it was time to discard my life of leisure and start looking for gainful employment.

Through the grapevine I'd heard a local builder was taking on apprentices and wasn't too fussy when it came to qualifications. So after a half-hearted pleading phone call, I became an apprentice electrician, working 40 hours a week for what seemed like an astronomical sum of £25. I now had £15 a week to spend on whatever took my fancy; more beer, more cigarettes and the odd vinyl record. I mention the records because, like so many others my age, they were to play a huge part in my early life.

With all the disposable cash I now had, I set about spending as much of it as I could: a habit I seem to

PUNKS ON SCOOTERS

have clung to till this day.

One Saturday in 1976, as I was walking aimlessly through Yate shopping centre I noticed a sign for a new record shop, tucked away over a men's outfitters. Mounting the stairs I found myself in what was probably the smallest record shop I'd ever seen, As I browsed through the limited amount of stock, I noticed a large poster on the wall announcing the release of a new single by a band I'd never heard of. I was intrigued by the artwork because it was like nothing I'd ever seen before. As I turned to leave I noticed the 'cheap bin'; a small cardboard box usually placed on the counter, full of forgotten seven-inch vinyl records or singles as they were more commonly known, which the owner had struggled to sell, even after they had been reduced.

Not one to turn my nose up at a bargain, I thumbed nonchalantly through the records, reciting my usual mantra, "Shit, shit, shit, Abba shit, shit, shit, Eagles shit... Umm not sure, shit, shit, shit."

'Not sure' was usually a sign that whatever it was, had grabbed my attention for some reason; maybe an interesting sleeve, or some group I'd heard of but had never listened to. On that fateful day my 'not sure' moment quickly turned into a purchase when I realised the record in my hand was the very same one that I'd noticed advertised on the poster moments before. I didn't realise it at the time but what I had in my hand was a piece of vinyl history that would go on to be one of the most important records ever released. It was by a strangely named band called The Sex Pistols. And the record? Well of course it was the era-defining 'Anarchy in the UK'. Not only did I leave the shop with the single but the poster as well, as the owner said I could have it if I bought the two remaining copies of 'Anarchy'. (I hate to think what they would be worth now as I'm sure the poster itself would be worth a small fortune... wherever it is).

My turntable hadn't seen much action for a while, with the charts dominated by the likes of the aforementioned Abba and the insipid Eagles. I can remember this all very clearly as I can still recall the smell of the dust around the valves burning away as I started up my long-neglected Dansette record player. I suppose it could have just as easily been any other of the punk records being released about that time, but my own punk epiphany was brought on by Johnny Rotten and his disparate band mates.

Britain in 1977 was long overdue a musical enema. For some time the charts had become swamped with middle of the road acts such as Johnny Mathis, Demis Roussos, Barry Manilow and the dreary Eagles.

So the discovery of 'Anarchy' and not forgetting the excellent 'I Wanna Be Me' on the B side, set me, and a few of my friends off on a musical journey that was both exciting and sometimes quite frightening. I became a punk rocker...

Without the internet, our main sources of information as to what was happening musically in the heartlands of England and 3000 miles away in America would come from weekly music papers such as *Sounds* and the vastly superior *New Musical Express*. Sporadic articles started to appear about bands playing in London venues such as the 100 Club and the Roundhouse. These bands included the New York-based groups that we had read about but were yet to hear let alone see live; bands such as the New York Dolls, Ramones and the excellent Television.

Within a few months it was clear that these bands were playing music with an attitude and sound that seemed a million miles away from anything that the very safe, controlling British music business had to offer. This musical revolution with its own intimidating and outrageous image for a brief moment in time went on to change the face of not only the British music scene and beyond, but appeared to threaten the whole fabric of the British way of life.

When The Sex Pistols managed to outrage the establishment and much of the world, or so it seemed at the time, with their four letter outbursts on the Today show presented by Bill Grundy, everything seemed to change. Grundy had obviously got them on his evening programme to make a point, but hadn't realised he was in fact playing into their hands, or Malcolm McLaren's.

The national outrage and condemnation spread quickly, perpetuated by the newspapers and TV Stations, which from our point of view had the opposite effect. We weren't outraged at all. In fact we saw it as our 'call to arms', just as the teddy boys had in the 1950s and the modernists in the 1960s. But there was a price to pay. Very quickly a wave of hate spread across the country directed at anything punk.

When Johnny Rotten was slashed several times across his arm, outside the Pegasus public house in Stoke Newington by a gang of men in their thirties, it seemed to escalate the hatred; almost condoning any abuse and violence that was levelled at punk and its followers. Every time you went out, you never knew if you were going to be harassed or attacked, which in some strange way made it all the more exciting.

Rural Frampton Cotterell and nearby Winterbourne weren't exactly the epicentre of the burgeoning Bristol punk scene and certainly didn't seem to complement the anarchistic stance we were trying to take with our 'outrageous clothing'. In the early days of punk, we wore clothing such as drainpipe jeans, leather jackets with safety pins attached, Inter-Giant baseball boots, winkle picker shoes, and even donkey jackets which seemed incredibly anti-establishment, especially with a few badges pinned on here and there decrying any sort of capitalism or promoting anarchy.

Suddenly there seemed to be an explosion of groups playing somewhere nearly every night; kids out of pure frustration from all over the country were now taking the lead from such groups as The Sex Pistols and The Clash picking up the guitar, learning a few chords and forming bands, some good, some bad, some very bad.

I can still remember The Buzzcocks, 999 and the Slits at Tiffany's, the Clash at the Exhibition Center (probably the most scary gig I ever attended, not because of the band but more because of the intimidating audience), Siouxie and The Banshees, Generation X and The Boomtown Rats at Stars and Stripes, (Siouxie finished the show after a couple of encores with the memorable lines 'how come you like us and the record companies don't?' which was all very confusing as she had opened the show decrying any sort of record contract or artistic sell out).

We saw Iggy Pop (he was going to commit suicide on stage, according to the rumour mill), The Damned, Elvis Costello, Stiff Little Fingers (seven encores) and so many others at the New Bristol Centre. We very nearly got to see the Sex Pistols at the Bamboo Club after queuing for hours one cold December evening, those that were lucky enough to get in, then qualified to buy a ticket for the following week... all went well until the night before the gig, when the club owned by Tony Bullimore burned down.

Bristol had its own punk bands such as The Undead, The Pigs, The Cortinas and Vice Squad, who managed to help sell out the Bristol Locarno when a rumour started to circulate that lead singer Beki Bondage was going to perform naked. These were exciting times for a seventeen-year-old.

Everybody seemed to hate us but 'we didn't care', to paraphrase Johnny Rotten.

Eventually the excitement died down as many of the groups sold out to the larger record companies. What had started out as a sort of socialist movement seemed to turn into a very capitalist one. Even the people that wanted to kill us just a few months before, were now popping into HMV and Virgin Records to get the latest releases from the bands that we had championed, like The Jam, The Clash and of course the ever-popular Stranglers.

By 1978 it was all over. Some of the bands went on to bigger and better things, (although I suspect some of them look back now at those pioneering days as probably the best they ever had). Some limped along and went back to the pub circuit, whilst others disappeared altogether.

For a while it was like we were in a wilderness, roaming aimlessly without any compass to show us the way. We had tasted excitement and we wanted more. With the big record companies once again calling the shots, New Wave was a sort of housewives' favourites version of punk. There were tunes in there somewhere; it just needed a good producer to bring them out. Gone was the raw excitement, only to be replaced with very much of what we had before.

Music and fashion have always fuelled most youth movements, but what was the chance another would come along in time to stop us becoming 'normal' again?

PUNKS ON SCOOTERS

By late 1978, I was living at a friend's house just across the river from my rather nice middle-class family home. Doug, my friend from school, had graciously offered me somewhere to stay, after I had had a somewhat one-sided fist fight with my rather unlikeable stepfather; a fight I now suspect he initiated to get me out. At the time I thought it was all my idea, as I stormed out of the house announcing, "That's it! I'm leaving. Fuck off!" not realising the irony; it was me that was 'fucking off' and had nowhere to go.

Doug was also a punk, and a very good one. He collected all the new vinyl releases with a dedication and planning that would have put the preparations for the D-Day landings to shame. I remember that we would sit in his front room, with a copy of *Sounds* or *NME* music papers, and would meticulously scrutinise the recent releases, writing down a long list of all the ones he thought worthy of being in his ever-growing collection.

Frampton Cotterell is a good ten miles from Bristol, where Virgin Records had recently opened a new store in Broadmead, after outgrowing their previous premises in Haymarket Walk in the Bearpit near the central bus station. Doug, in true punk fashion was unemployed at the time, and didn't actually have any transport except for the bus. Doug's mother, on the other hand, had a car and worked in Brunswick Square, a short walk to the newly opened Virgin Records. So she was the obvious solution to his logistical problem; actually getting the records.

I've never mentioned it to Doug, but I've always been amused by the thought of his 50-year-old mother standing in line with all the leather-clad mohican punks, especially when she would get to the counter and start reading off the rather long list.

"Young man, have you got The Pigs – 'Youthanasia', The Undead – 'It's Corruption', 999 – 'Homicide'? And I'll take the new one by Wayne County, you knowe the one... 'If you don't want to...'"

"Umm, yes madam. Anything else?"

"No that's all thank you. Oh, any idea when the new Sid Vicious record will be in stock? The one where he sings that nice Frank Sinatra song?"

Still makes me smile.

Doug's house was full of music. If the record player wasn't banging out some recently released new wave or reggae track, then his mum would have the transistor radio on in the kitchen. Although the new wave music wasn't that bad, it really was a poor substitute for the raw energy of early punk.

We devoured *New Musical Express* and *Sounds* weekly from cover to cover in the hope that something new and exciting might be coming our way. I suppose in these days of on-demand information, it seems strange that we would have to wait, sometimes up to a month, to find out anything that wasn't mainstream happening on the music scene, especially in London. And then it seemed another six months before it filtered down to us in the provinces, especially fashion.

The building trade took a terrible dive during

Jim Callaghan's 'winter of discontent' and I found myself on the dole once again. Not much had changed, but I did sense a renewed vigour in the work-weary staff's expectations of me actually looking for some kind of employment. This was a whole new approach. Previously the game plan was to let the work find you, rather than to actively seek it out. Sitting in the dole office every other Tuesday, I was frequently assured by the seasoned 'doleys' that the country was going to 'rack and ruin' and the old ways of doing things were much better. "The job should find you, not you find the job", they would say, almost in unison.

Who was I to argue with these seasoned professionals? After all they had more than 10 years' experience behind them. I on the other hand was a mere novice.

My father had been in the Royal Navy and I suddenly felt the urge to travel the world at the government's expense. Even if there was a war, the chance of me getting hit by a missile 2,000 miles out at sea was quite slim, or so I thought.

I'd been informed by the nice man in the forces recruitment office that it would take about six months before I would actually start my basic training as a naval air mechanic. All I had to do was pass a few exams, including the medical. For some reason the medical was the part of the process I was least looking forward to. I had always had a bad self-image, being quite small and skinny and quite self conscious, so the thought of stripping off and jumping around in front of some complete stranger filled me with utter dread. Especially as I had heard you had to climb a rope 'just like a monkey', something I didn't really feel comfortable with.

As the day approached the first thing to climb was my anxiety levels, but with my new mantra 'What would Kojak do?' I travelled into Bristol city centre to join my future shipmates aboard the HMS Recruitment Office. Stripped down to our underpants we all stood in line shivering in the cold hallway before we were individually called into a small, well-equipped gymnasium-type room.

I entered and the first thing I saw was the dreaded exercise rope, hanging mockingly from the ceiling. To my right was a figure bending over a table, writing something in what I could only assume was probably his version of a ship's log. As he straightened up, it became clear he was well over six feet tall, wearing a white coat, and with a stethoscope around his neck. As he turned to greet me, my heart lifted as I noticed he was sporting the thickest-lensed glasses I had ever seen this side of Les Dawson's character Cosmo Smallpiece. From that point on, my confidence started to grow as I realised this man probably couldn't see his clipboard, let alone me.

"Right, let me listen to your lungs... aha ok" he said.

"Now drop your underwear and bend over. Uh hu... uh hu... hmm. Okay, all seems in order."

"Well that's a plus," I thought.

He put the cold stethoscope on my chest. "Hmm,

that's strange."

"What is?' I asked.

"Give me 20 press-ups," he said.

At this point my confidence was starting to slowly wane, but I was still buoyed up by the knowledge that he couldn't actually see me in my underwear, or if he did it was most probably something of a foggy blur. Once again he placed the cold stethoscope on my chest. "Hmm, hang on. I won't be a minute."

As the door closed behind him, I stood there half-naked in my underwear, feeling more vulnerable than at any other time in my life. Suddenly the door opened, and in came two other medical officers closely followed by two rather attractive young nurses, all staring at me.

This really wasn't going to plan. I was hoping to get through all this with as little fuss as possible.

"Right give me ten star jumps," he said.

"Hmm... Now drop and give me ten press-ups."

After listening to my heart again, they all moved into a huddle and started to confer. Minutes passed as each one seemed to voice their opinion followed by a cursory glance in my direction.

"Is there a problem?" I timidly asked.

"Well yes and no" he confusingly replied.

"It's okay. Umm, look you have a heart flutter, but it seems to go away when you are exercising, so don't worry about it."

"Oh great! Can I go now please?"

"Yes. That's it," he replied and handed me a piece of paper.

As I made an Olympic dash for the door that Dr Roger Bannister would have been proud of, he shouted after me, "Oh hang on, come back. You haven't done the rope yet."

"Oh, shit!" I muttered, I thought I had got away with it. Would this hell ever end!

As I climbed the dreaded rope, I could feel all their eyes intently focused on my semi-naked body. Defeated and exhausted, I inched up the rope with what energy I could muster, thinking to myself 'what could any of this have to do with fixing bloody helicopters?'

As it turned out I never did find out the answer. Coerced by the dole office, I had taken a day's work at an engineering company in Yate. The day's work soon turned into weeks then months then years, after the managers convinced me that I had a bright and shiny future ahead of me, and that I'd be a fool to pass up such an opportunity. Yes, I was indeed a fool. I believed them.

Looking back with the benefit of hindsight, maybe it wasn't such a bad thing, I'd been struggling with the thought of saying 'Aye Aye Sir' on dry land for some time, and I suspected that I would have been the one tied naked to the hot radiator, for not taking seriously all the discipline and honour of serving Her Majesty the Queen. Old habits die hard, and trying to be the class clown when you're supposed to be ensuring the air crews' safety probably wasn't going to be a match made in heaven.

I'm pretty sure I wouldn't have had such a great

time and made so many friends in the Navy, as I did being part of the mod revival when it burst onto the British music scene, spawning several hundred scooter clubs and mod bands up and down the country. Maybe the whole idea of joining the Royal Navy was just a way of getting out of the dole queue, and me wanting 'to be someone'

Chapter 2

THE MOD REVIVAL

If 1976 was the year of punk, then 1979 was the year of the mod revival, although its roots can be traced back to 1978 in London, it really took off with the cinema release of the now cult film *Quadrophenia*, based on The Who's album of the same name. I suspect that prior to 1979, I didn't really have much of a clue what a mod was or wasn't, or if I did, it was a vague image of some feminine looking blokes parading around Carnaby Street in the mid to late 1960s. I'm not entirely sure why I wanted to become one, although I suspect it was because I had become so used to the excitement generated by the early punk bands and being part of a tribe; I was just desperate for the next exciting 'something' to come along.

The mod revival didn't explode onto the music scene the way that punk had, it appeared more gradually, almost with a politeness that was probably more befitting its tailored image than the anarchistic safety-pin brashness of the punk explosion. My first experience of its growing popularity came one evening in 1978 when I went to Bristol with some friends to see The Numbers, a local four-piece punk band from Yate, just up the road from Winterbourne.

Trinity Church in Old Market had become a popular venue for many different types of bands, especially punk and reggae and in later years was to host such unknowns as Duran Duran and U2. The night started quite strangely as we walked towards the old converted church, when my friend Steve accidently stood on a couple having sex in the long grass in the disused graveyard. It was rumoured the girl was later thrown out of Fairfax House department store after getting caught having sex in the photobooth on the ground floor with a completely different guy..

  As we entered the church it was obvious this wasn't going to be a good evening. There seemed to be a new gang in town, a gang that looked pretty menacing. With their pork pie hats, green army-issue parkas, and Paul Weller-style narrow sunglasses, these guys were mod revivalists, and although a few months previously they had been punks themselves, now they were our sworn enemy (even though we didn't know at the time). The tension throughout the evening could be cut with a knife as the outnumbered punks congregated to the left of the stage with what turned out to be the Barton Hill mods to the right. As the night wore on, the feeling that something was going to happen, was ramped up when a beer glass came crashing down onto the floor in front of us nearly hitting Steve's girlfriend. This was the first of many nights of violence I was to witness at Trinity, in town and in the suburbs.

  I remember travelling down the M32 motorway in a friend's car one evening on the way to the Locarno, with the radio blaring out, and hearing John Peel introduce a new band from Coventry called The Specials, with their debut 7-inch single 'Gangsters'. I think it's probably best to let John Peel explain exactly what it was like hearing this song for the first time.

"That was The Specials 'Gangsters'. One of those records that really changes your life. I mean it actually does, rather like I suppose The Damned's first single, where you wake up the next day and nothing's ever really quite the same again."

And as John so succinctly pointed out, nothing for me 'was really quite the same again' I had finally found that 'something'.

The Specials really did seem different, like nothing we had heard before, it was the sort of music that got your feet tapping, and want to get up and dance as soon as you heard it. With their pork pie hats and tonic suits, not only did they look sharp but they also had songs that seemed to be more socially aware, especially from a working class point of view.

The band were formed by Coventry-based Jerry Dammers, whose dad Horace Dammers was Dean of Bristol Cathedral from 1973-1987. Jerry went to school in Coventry and met the rest of the band there so Bristol can't really claim any part of The Specials. The band secured a deal with Chrysalis Records, which paved the way for the formation of the 2 Tone label that is still synonymous with skinheads, rude boys and mod revivalists.

With The Specials leading the 2 Tone vanguard, other bands such as The Beat, Body Snatchers,

Selecter and of course Madness, for a brief moment seemed like they were being carried along by The Specials' success. Although Madness were to go on to be more commercially successful than the other bands with their cheeky chappy version of ska, it was The Specials that gave the whole ska revival its respectability.

Around this time two groups seemed to come from nowhere and became the first mod revival bands to get into the charts and appear on *Top of the Pops*. First to release a record was the quite dreadfully named Merton Parkas with their equally quite dreadful debut single 'You Need Wheels' which you would have thought was at least going to promote the use of every mod's favourite mode of transport the scooter, but oh no, not for these boys from London's Merton Park, (see what they did there? Park... Parkas) it was the car for them, after all according to Mick Talbot the lead singer, if you wanted 'to go far, you needed a car' and if for some unfathomable reason you needed to 'do deals' then apparently 'you needed wheels' (I'm still not quite sure what deals they were actually doing, although I have a sneaky suspicion it was more that it rhymed with wheels than for any financial gain or illicit drug acquisition).

This wasn't a very auspicious start for a movement that was hoping to garner some sort of musical credibility. I can only imagine what bands such as The Chords, Squire and The Purple Hearts must have thought when they heard that this dreadful record had somehow managed to get into the charts, making them in the eyes of the public, guilty by association.

The next band to break out were The Lambrettas from East Sussex with a cover version of the 1950s Coasters song 'Poison Ivy'. The Lambrettas had signed to Elton John's Rocket label which it would appear could afford a better producer than the Merton Parkas' label Beggars Banquet. The Lambrettas, in my opinion, actually came up with a well-produced record much better than the original, although their stage appearance seemed to be lacking in any sort of 'cool' that was supposed to be associated with the mod movement. To me they always seemed to look more like a bunch of Gerry Anderson puppets that had consumed just a little too much speed.

Neither song really captured the feel or excitement that we as mods thought the revival deserved; it was only when Secret Affair released 'Time for Action' that we actually felt there was indeed some musical substance, which the ska movement seemed to have in abundance. With the single reaching number 17 on the charts, Secret Affair found themselves at the forefront of the mod revival. Only too happy to take on the mantle, Ian Page managed to alienate himself and the band from a great deal of the record-buying public, by proclaiming himself with an air of arrogance the spokesman for a generation, without any consultation with the people he claimed to represent.

I'd never really differentiated between the 2 Tone ska music, and the angry young man music from the likes of The Jam, The Chords and Purple Hearts, to me it was all the same, just part of the 80s mod movement. It's only now I can look back and see that it wasn't one movement at all, it was several, all coming together at the same time drawing on past influences and trying to create something new.

Much has been written about The Jam spearheading the mod revival, especially with their career saving album release *All Mod Cons*. But for us The Jam with Paul Weller's song writing skills was just a nice addition to something that had been growing organically for some time. The likes of Secret Affair, The Chords, and even Bristol's own Mayfair were to us, exciting and new; The Jam had been around since the beginning of punk and were already regarded as some kind of musical elder statesmen. The Jam certainly were a great asset to the mod revival, as they gave it some sort of musical legitimacy, but with or without them it would still have happened, but to what degree is of course debatable.

As I mentioned earlier, I had grown up in the rather nice middle class area of Winterbourne just outside Bristol.

Winterbourne in those days was a quiet village where professional footballers and their managers all seemed to live and eventually retire. The Ridings High School that also served the neighbouring areas of Frampton Cotterell, Coalpit Heath and Hambrook was situated on the High Street, flanked by green playing fields, tennis courts, and a large well-kept duck pond. The Ridings as far as I remember up until 1977 was notable for... absolutely nothing.

Pupils very rarely went into higher or further education, preferring to get apprenticeships or follow their parents into lifelong careers in financial services or the building trade. I only mention this because the area seemed to spawn more than its fair share of budding musicians. One or two of the pupils seemed to have that special something that separated the wannabes from the truly gifted...

Rebecca Louise Bond was a sweet, quiet pupil who would go on to alter the face of punk music when she changed her name to Beki Bondage and fronted the seminal Bristol punk band Vice Squad. After signing to Riot City Records, they had reasonable chart success which enabled them to travel the world to sell-out concerts, probably throw some televisions out of hotel windows, and secure numerous appearances on the covers of many influential music tabloids of the day, such as *Melody Maker*, *NME*, *Smash Hits* and *Sounds*.

Beki had championed another punk band from the Ridings that went by the name The Undead. Through her influence she had managed to secure them a record deal also on the Riot City record label. Produced by the ubiquitous Steve Street, their 7-inch single 'It's Corruption' secured a very healthy chart placing at number 18 on the Indie charts, and their later release 'Sanctuary' was included in the

Riot City compilation Riotous Assembly reaching number nine on the Indie Album Chart.

But the success of these two bands was to pale into insignificance when compared to the stellar success of Wayne Hussey and The Mission. I remember Wayne always carrying his guitar around with him at school but looking the most unlikely person to succeed in any shape or form as a pop star. Wayne was a quiet and very likeable fellow pupil and played in the school hall several times to the great delight of his fellow classmates. After he left school, Wayne became a trainee manager at the Co-Op in Coalpit Heath, where I assume the dreams of becoming a professional musician and a desire to be someone, gave him the drive to pack it all in, and move to Liverpool. After brief stints with Pauline Murray & The Invisible Girls, Dead or Alive and The Sisters of Mercy, Wayne formed his own band The Mission and went on to sell huge numbers of albums worldwide.

So when the music scene once again took a whole new direction with the mod revival, it wasn't too much of a surprise that the Ridings High School would produce a band that wasn't only good, but also fun.

I had known Mike Darby for several years and he always came across as a 'go getting' sort of guy, so it didn't seem much of a surprise when I heard he had formed a band straight after leaving school called Mike and The Mole Men. I can't actually remember what they sounded like or if I ever even saw them, but I suspect they had more enthusiasm than musical talent. The band soon broke up, and I heard, that it was one of those rare occasions when the band through complete despondency couldn't even be bothered to cite musical differences. His next band however The Rimshots was a more palatable affair with the gifted fellow pupil Michael 'Fuzz' Furzeman on guitar and Mike Darby once again trying his best on vocals – I'm sure Mike would admit that his singing was more enthusiasm than ability, but then it's easy to knock someone when you haven't got the guts to get up there and do it yourself.

Live, The Rimshots were a great five-piece band, playing predominantly ska music and quickly managed to secure a core mod following and a recording contract with Shoc Wave Records, with whom they released a very fine debut single 'I Was Wrong', coupled with 'Stuck in a Boat', written by another Ridings pupil Greg Embury. The band went on to support The Body Snatchers, Hazel O'Connor as well as The Beat.

Chapter 3

THE CALL OF CARNABY STREET

Living for the weekend has always been an intrinsic part of the 'mod way of life'. But for those of us living in the suburbs during the later months of 1979, it wasn't so much that we spent our time in some dedicated night club every Saturday, dancing into the early hours, popping Purple Hearts or Blues, but more that we would catch the bus into Bristol's Broadmead, and do some shopping, in the hope of finding clothes that could pass as 'mod acceptable'.

To anyone that has any doubts as to the importance of clothes to a mod, I can only explain it this way. There are only three things that really matter in the whole wide world, scooters, music and clothes. Whichever order of importance you choose to put them in, is entirely a personal choice.

Charity shops were always a good place to find such things as button-down shirts, 16-inch bottom trousers and three-button jackets, items that were almost impossible to find in the usual men's outfitters, unless you had enough money to get something made to measure.

Personally I tried to keep away from the charity shops as in those days they were quite dank and grubby places, unlike the more upmarket ones of today. A lot of the clothes had a smell that never seemed to go away even after cleaning, which was very similar to the Army surplus stores which supplied the parkas, and much later on combat trousers, flight jackets, jump suits and monkey boots.

I'd brushed with 'sharp' fashion several years earlier when coming of age and beginning my secondary education at The Ridings, in 1971. Fashion until then hadn't really been that important to me, although I had always liked to keep myself neat and tidy, taking an admiring lead from my rather dapper, frequently absent, father – although I did draw the line when he enthusiastically tried to encourage me several years later to wear some of his hand-me-down safari suits.

Although a little intimidating, my first day at 'the big school', as it was known, wasn't as embarrassing as I had initially anticipated. I was very nearly the only boy in the school wearing shorts other than for PE when my new long trousers mysteriously went missing from our clothes line, only to be found some days later in next door's dog basket.

I had been assigned to the rather uninspiring Wesley House which was more renowned for its formidable Housemaster Mr Johnstone or 'Pegleg' as he was surreptitiously known, than for any scholastic achievements. As I nervously entered the front doors the whole building was alive with the nervous chatter and excitement of fellow newbies and seasoned pupils returning from the long joyous summer holidays.

Despite being surrounded by strangers, I did notice

a few familiar faces, either from my old junior school or those that I had seen frequenting the local parks and playing fields. Craig had also attended Elm Park Juniors; although he was not someone I had had many dealings with, except on the odd occasion or should I say 'altercation'. Craig was one of those boys that, although small in stature, certainly made up for it with the size of his ego and seemed to take great delight in the suffering of others: man or animal, with the odd bit of vandalism thrown in for good measure.

It would appear much had changed over the summer holidays as Craig had taken to emulating his older brother who had become a skinhead the previous year. Craig wore the unmistakable 'uniform' of Dr Marten boots, Ben Sherman buttoned-down shirt, tight Levi jeans with braces and customary close-cropped hair. Craig, it seemed, took great delight in seeing me on that first day at school, not as I suspected because he was happy to see me, but more so that he could showboat his new shiny thirteen-hole orthopaedic footwear. Craig was very proud that he had a brand new pair of Dr Martens and took great delight in the fact that I didn't.

These Dr Martens would became quite famous around school for a short while, when for some inexplicable reason Craig thought it a good idea to 'christen them' by kicking in the Wesley House toilet door. His shiny 'bovver' boot became stuck as it passed through to the other side. The more he struggled the more it became wedged. This obviously wasn't the most auspicious start to Craig's academic year, especially because one of the house masters had to help get him released.

This unfortunate encounter with Craig was the start of my own fashion awakening leading to my whole new look which began with the purchase of black leather-soled, tasselled loafers manufactured in Bristol by Lennards. It was essential to complete the look with aftermarket quarter-inch tips on the heels and Blakey's 'segs' (small metal studs that pushed into the shoe's sole) for that extra military crunching sound as you walked around the school passageways. The Blakey's not only produced a great sound like a sergeant major on a parade ground but had the added effect of causing a myriad of wonderful sparks when you were riding your push bike and trailing your feet on the ground behind you.

Wrangler blue Sta Press were my trouser of choice, managing to stay pressed, not because of some secret treatment in the manufacturing process, but more I suspect because they were actually made from some sort of woven plastic material. The material had the very strange habit of melting, rather than ripping, when grazed along the tarmac after falling off your push bike or when playing football. All this was topped off with a knitted tank top, purple and black striped socks, white Ben Sherman shirt and reversible black or tartan Harrington jacket.

So when the mod revival came along I felt really

PUNKS ON SCOOTERS

comfortable with a look that seemed in part similar to what I had worn several years earlier.

Unlike the more adventurous Punk era, the mod revival had a more defined set of rules. These rules would change dramatically within a few years with the rise of the scooter boy, when the focus became more the scooter than the previously mentioned 'holy trinity' of 'clothes, scooters and music'. In the early days the main influence was more a ska revival style, with pork pie hats, black suits, white socks, buttoned-down shirts and tasselled loafer shoes. None of this was strictly mod as our dress sense was heavily influenced by sharp-dressed bands such as The Specials, The Bodysnatchers, The Selecter and Madness, 2 Tone bands that seemed to be appearing on *Top of the Pops* so much, it seemed almost pointless owning a colour TV.

And to be honest it was after all a mod revival, not a mod recreation, admittedly a lot of us didn't care about the finer details of the movement we were now part of as long as we were having a good time. Many of us were initially just punks on scooters. As long as it was exciting and fun then that was good enough for us.

As the British media became more and more aware of what was happening in terms of youth culture, articles started to appear in the mainstream papers and magazines, it became quite clear that what we thought was a mod look and what we had been wearing, was some way adrift from each other.

When Pete Townsend's company Eel Pie Productions

published *Mods!* by Richard Barnes at the tail end of 1979, we suddenly had in our hands what we thought was the 'Bible' for all things modernist. With articles on how to walk, drink, ride a scooter and even stand, this was a real eye opener for any teenager that wanted to sit astride a scooter and be the envy of his pedestrian mates.

Now we knew how to do it properly...

Doug my friend had embraced being a mod with the same enthusiasm and dedication that he had shown several years earlier when punk had exploded onto the music scene. He had managed to obtain the best American-issue fishtail parka I'd ever seen which fitted him perfectly. American-issue fishtail parkas were extremely sought after compared to the German 'short' ones or the the green 'gas mask cape with hood'.

Doug truly was a sight to behold with razor-sharp creases in his tonic trousers, blue Harrington jacket, pork pie hat, perfectly-pressed button down shirt, and brogue shoes, shined to a standard any Queen's Guard would be proud of. Not only did he look good, but he also knew how to carry himself, and with his James Dean good looks and perfected poses, he was a major contender to be the Bristol 'Face' of 1979.

If there was a secret to Doug's transformation from punk rocker to 'mod about town' then it was that he had an eye for the finer details in choosing his clothes, and had made a huge effort to become one of Bristol's best-dressed mods. We mere mortals, on the other hand, could only aspire to what Doug seemed to so effortlessly achieve.

  Any information about a place selling mod clothing was usually closely guarded, (especially after one embarrassing evening when everyone turned up wearing exactly the same blue pinstripe, button-down shirt they had all got from Keith Pople's). Doug had heard that a new shop had opened just off of Bristol's main shopping centre, selling the sort of clothes that had been very much sought after, and until now in very short supply. As we sat on the top deck of the bus one Saturday morning, Frampton Cotterell faded from our thoughts such was the excitement of what might await us.

  On the way, Doug confided that the 'secret' mod shop was in fact called 'Heroes', situated half way up Union Street near Castle Park. After arriving at the Bristol Bus Station we quickly made our way down the steps that led to the Bear Pit, passing the once popular punk clothing shop Paradise Garage, then onto Broadmead shopping centre. As we approached the Odeon cinema on that sunny Saturday morning, fate dealt a hand that was going to change everything I did over the next four years. In the distance I could hear the unmistakable sound of a two-stroke engine coming towards us. Turning the corner I was met with what I thought was probably the most beautiful sight I had ever seen. There in front of us, outside Heroes, were two Vespa scooters, just being parked up by two very cool looking mods, who were sporting Fred Perry polo shirts, sta prest trousers and tassel loafers.

There was the unmistakeable sweet smell of two stroke oil in the air, a smell that gets in to the veins of any aspiring mod. From that moment on I knew that there was nothing else in the world that I wanted more than my very own Italian scooter, one that would most probably require a great deal of renovation and mechanical know how, considering my very meagre budget.

Heroes was certainly worth the visit because it was the first time we had found somewhere selling the sort of clothes that we had seen the London-based mods and 2 Tone bands wearing. There were tonic suits of all colours, buttoned-down shirts, coats, jumpers and even The Jam-style shoes. Looking around I noticed a nice dark blue slim fit jumper, similar to the Fred Perry ones, but reassuringly just that little bit more expensive. After handing over my hard-earned cash I was more than happy with the day's outcome, because not only had we discovered a clothes shop that sold the sort of clothing we were after, but I'd also managed to get a rather nifty jumper to wear on my Italian scooter if I ever managed to get one.

The jumper very quickly became my pride and joy, but sadly was to come to a very sticky end not long after I bought it. As I was standing at the bar of the Locarno one night chatting to Vespa Vince, some guy brushed past. Slowly moving among the closely knit crowd saying his hellos and acknowledging familiar faces, he seemed to be followed by a very strange thin luminous light, tracking his every move. We watched intently as he wove in and out of the crowd, looking like something out of Greek mythology, conjuring up images of when Theseus entered the labyrinth to kill the Minotaur. The mystery deepened as he seemed to be completely oblivious to what was happening all around him. That is until everything became very clear as Vince laughed out loud and knowingly nudged me, pointing with great delight at my new prized jumper as it was unravelling at great speed before our very eyes…

Even though more and more mod-style clothing was starting to appear on the Bristol streets, there was nothing like a good shopping trip along the M4 to London. These trips were always greeted with a lot of excitement and anticipation, especially if it involved travelling to Carnaby Street and its famous 60s-themed shops. For a few pounds per head, a coach would be organised and quickly packed with a bunch of over-excited parka-wearing teenagers, all travelling to the capital city to savour the fashion delights of the West End.

Carnaby Street had been the focal point of all things mod in the 1960s and although still on the outside a vibrant place, on the inside it had been slowly decaying, desperately trying to hold on to its past glories but selling poor-quality tat.

With the release of *Quadrophenia* in the cinemas Carnaby Street was experiencing a bit of a renaissance by cashing in on all things 60s and mod. Gone were the love beads and Afghan coats, to be replaced with MA1 flight jackets, Jam shoes, parkas and nearly any product you could possibly imagine that could carry a Union Jack emblem.

According to an *NME* advert, Carnaby Cavern was the place Paul Weller and other members of The Jam got their suits made. The advert proudly announced 'WE MAKE FOR: The Jam, Secret Affair, Joe Jackson, The Specials, Back to Zero, The Crooks, and many more, SO WHY NOT YOU?'

Why not indeed? We thought, as we disembarked from the coach and made our way to what would most probably be the highlight of the day. The shop on the outside was all we could have hoped for with a huge Union jack flag banner over the door, nice sharp suits in the window, photos of The Jam and The Pleasers cut out of Record Mirror, Fab 208 and Jackie magazines stuck all over the windows.

The London-based Pleasers were a band that have been rather forgotten now, although more associated with power pop, they seemed (from a distance) to fit in quite nicely with the mod revival. With their mop-top haircuts, Beatles-style suits and Cuban-heeled boots, they had released a few records and scored pretty well in the charts with a cover of the Who's 'The Kids Are All Right', albeit done in their own Merseybeat style that they claimed was 'Thames Beat'.

Inside the Carnaby Cavern we were surrounded by various items of mod clothing: £40 for a jacket, £20 for a pair of trousers (either off-the-peg or made-to-measure). The shop was full of the finest tailoring I had ever seen (not that I was an expert by any stretch of the imagination); all worthy of my hard earned £60. After all, why go to Carnaby Street if you're not going to get a 'real head-turner' of a suit?

There I was, like a child in a sweet shop, after travelling 120 miles up the M4 with a coach full of excitable teenage mods, all hoping to find the one piece of clothing that would make the journey a true success. There were Union Jack jackets 'just like the one Paul Weller and the rest of the Jam wears', mohair suits 'just like the ones Secret Affair wear' and tonic suits, yes you've got it, 'just like The Specials wear'.

So what did I do? For some unfathomable reason I ordered myself a made-to-measure exact copy of the suit that Paul McCartney wore in 'A Hard Day's Night'; completely shapeless, in a grey nylon-type material (not unlike the material used in my indestructible sta-press) with a bit of black velvet on the collar.

Maybe for some brief moment I felt an emotional release after I had come clean about my Fab Four fixation, or was it that my childhood dream of in fact being a Beatle became too much to subdue? Whatever the reason, I can only assume that it was brought on by seeing The Pleasers photographs moments before stuck on the shop window, re-enacting their very own little Beatles love affair. It would seem that for a brief moment in 1979 my biggest claim to fame was that I was the only one-man Beatles tribute act in Bristol, if not the whole of the United Kingdom. The suit was soon discarded after visiting Lourdes nightclub in Fairfax Street. I knew my fashion statement a little was too wide of the mark when the woman at the reception desk earnestly assured me that fancy dress night was the week before.

Still in search of the elusive scooter, I would scour the *Bristol Evening Post* every day in the hope that not only would there be a Lambretta or Vespa for sale, but one within my very small budget.

In 1979 scooters were few and far between having been replaced by the more reliable Japanese motorbikes that had started to flood the British market. Most Lambrettas and Vespas were considered junk and only fit for the scrap heap and that's where thousands of them sadly ended up. Luckily for us, quite a few had been put into storage and duly forgotten about. With the resurgence of all things mod, more and more advertisements started to appear in the local papers as their owners realised that they now had a hot commodity tucked away gathering dust in the back of their garage or garden shed.

Doug's mum had kindly offered to stand the cost of my scooter and made it easy for me to pay her back over several months, interest free. After what seemed an eternity I finally acquired an LI125 Lambretta in much need of renovation, for the princely sum of £125, less side panels, which had apparently been removed sometime previously by its owner to block the holes in the garden fence where Airey Nieve the family rabbit had made several successful escape bids.

Nobody I knew seemed to have the first idea about how to take apart a Lambretta or restore one. Although mechanically sound, the paintwork was pretty bad and most of the electrics were rotten. Being the inquisitive type, I just had to strip it all down myself, repaint it, and hopefully solve the problem of getting it up and running and through the dreaded M.O.T.

Without a clue as to what I was doing, I went about stripping down my new Italian scooter and restoring it to some semblance of its former glory. Aplins on the Bath Road was one of the only shops in Bristol still supplying Lambretta spares. I use the term 'supplying' very loosely because after several visits over the summer I can't actually remember getting any of the parts I needed. I became convinced I was one of the most unlucky scooterists in the world. It seemed every time I went into the shop to get that certain part for my scooter, I was earnestly informed by the owner old man Aplin 'Sorry just sold the last one' or if he was in a more talkative mood 'See that bloke walking down there? He just had the last one'

For years afterwards I thought I had just had a terrible run of luck, only to be told on very good authority that the shop was so under stocked that Mr Aplin had come up with a set repertoire of sayings to deflect attention away from the fact he actually didn't have much of anything behind the counter.

This was the summer of '79. Doug had managed to join the West Side Unicorns Scooter Club without actually owning a scooter, securing a regular ride on the back of Jon Andrews' Lambretta. I, on the other hand, somewhat jealous at hearing his many enthralling stories of running battles with bikers and skinheads, had spent the whole time, when not at work, in his mum's garage, up to my neck in piles of aerosol cans, thinners and emery cloth, most of which I had acquired from my very generous although oblivious employers.

As soon as my scooter was ready and I'd worked out how to ride it... (This was a whole new experience from the FS1E DX Yamaha moped I'd been used to) I started accompanying Doug on his regular visits into Bristol. We would meet up with the Westside Unicorns at such places as The Greyhound pub in Broadmead and The Wagon & Horses on Stapleton Road or Nag's Head as it was known, due to the fact it was occasionally used for exterior filming of *Only Fools and Horses*.

The core members of the Westside Unicorns Scooter Club were the likes of Steve Dixon, Andy Nethercott, Rob 'The Job' Tucker, Foxy, John Andrews, Craig Dyer and Cockney Simon all of whom had grown up in the much 'harder' areas of Bristol such as Knowle West, Barton Hill, Whitchurch and the most feared of all Hartcliffe – a place guaranteed to put the fear of god into any teenager that didn't

PUNKS ON SCOOTERS

live there, due to its almost mythical status as the most violent place you could possibly imagine.

These guys didn't mess about; you knew exactly where you stood with them. It was all quite refreshing

Chapter 4

THE LOCARNO AND SUBURBAN VIOLENCE

The build-up, to an evening out on the town or to watch a band, was a painstaking one, involving preening, ironing and a lot of mirror checking. Once we were all ready to go, we would pile into Rich's car, and head down the M32 motorway towards Bristol with the radio cassette blaring out the likes of Secret Affair's 'Glory Boys' or 'Time for Action' music that really captured the excitement and elitism of the time, and certainly got you in the mood for a night out.

Our usual destination was the ABC New Bristol Centre in Frogmore Street a huge concrete entertainment complex, sitting on the site of what was once a small muddy lane, running under Park Street all the way up to College Green. It opened to much fanfare in 1966, with an ice skating rink, various dance halls and a cinema. With its state-of-the-art facilities it was soon attracting people from all over the South West and Wales.

For a teenager in the late 1970s it was a dream come true. If you were looking for a night out and lots of girls, then you were spoilt for choice. If you didn't want to spend the evening at the cinema or adjacent Cabot Bar on the ground floor you could climb the central concrete staircase, where you had a choice of venues, Raquel's Night Club and The

Locarno Ballroom on the first floor or the Mayfair Suite on the second which seemed to always be frequented by midlife crisis types wearing high-waisted trousers and spanish-looking frilly shirts.

For us, The Locarno was a great place. Most Saturday nights would be spent drinking and dancing to chart hits new and old with the addition of a house band that went by the rather confusing name of Chaos, a name more attributable to a punk band than the four blokes doddering around on stage looking more like an aging version of Smokie than a band that was going to cause any sort of anarchy.

The ballroom was huge, with a beautifully lit ceiling and several bars, including the self-contained Bali Hai, with its own sound system, dance floor and unrealistic plastic palm trees. Even when the Locarno was near to overflowing you could usually get quickly served a pint of watered down lager or a Pernod for the ladies in the now customary plastic glass (glass was replaced by plastic soon after the emergence of punk).

After a while it became more and more difficult to get past the bouncers on the doors, because they had become very wary of the rise in the new mod culture, and the reports of seaside violence that came with it. Anyone wearing white socks was turned away as the bouncers had been informed this was a sure way of spotting a mod trouble maker.

If you were lucky enough to have befriended one of the doormen you could usually get in, although this wasn't always assured, so a precautionary ploy of wearing black socks over the white one's usually did the trick. This was a testament to many a mod's dedication to style, because it would have been far easier just to have bitten the bullet and worn a darker shade of sock.

Once inside it was time to remove the over socks and strut around the building checking out what 'talent' was available. Although the girls seemed to be greatly outnumbered by the guys, there always seemed to be enough to go around. Fights would randomly break out throughout the night, fuelled by alcohol and jealousy, usually targeted at the mods who for that brief moment in time seemed to have become incredibly irresistible to the female clientele, partly due I'm sure to the sharp suits, white socks and menacing stares (sometimes obscured by very dark 'wrap around' sunglasses, which looked good, but almost rendered the wearer completely blind in the darkened corners of the night club).

It was around this time several of us became quite 'bladder retentive.' A necessity that ensured that however much you drank during the night you wouldn't have to use the toilet. The toilets were always a good place to get jumped by the kitters or casuals as we called them, who would wait their moment and follow you in, then take great delight in dragging you into a cubicle and giving you a good hiding for daring to be a mod.

Although fraught with many dangers, for a brief few months it was like being in mod nirvana, especially where girls were concerned. Anyone who was wearing anything resembling mod attire could do no wrong, and if for some strange reason the suit (and white socks) weren't working their magic we always brought along our secret weapon... Steve.

Steve was 5'10", blond haired and blue eyed, with the west coast look that any budding Californian surfer would be proud of. His success rate with women was truly phenomenal, he could sit for hours chatting, then announce that he was going to get a girlfriend and some 20 minutes later would return with his latest conquest on his arm. Steve definitely had 'a way with women' and with his many chat up lines and winning smile he seemed to have a 100 per cent success rate.

We all fed at the altar that was Steve, and when he got bored with his latest conquest, we were only too happy to console them and then take advantage of their vulnerability.

I had known Steve since we left school, not only did he have a keen interest in women, but also an almost obsessive fascination with Bruce Lee. I clearly remember leaving The Globe public house in Frampton Cotterell late one night quite drunk, when Steve decided to rush home and get his Nunchucks from his bedroom. For those unsure what a Nunchuck is, it was two bits of wood joined together with a piece of chain with which Bruce Lee dispatched many of his adversaries. Steve returned stripped to the waist and stood in the middle of the road facing the traffic as he gave a rather poor but pretty dangerous exhibition of his Nunchuck skill. As the cars started to back up the road in complete disbelief, I managed to convince him that this was all a bit odd, and it was probably time we went home.

Things really didn't go to plan when Steve offered me a deal. The only way he would stop, was if I would race him through his neighbours' front gardens. Each house had a small adjoining fence which could easily be cleared if enough speed had been gathered. Always up for a challenge I accepted, especially as Steve was sure to lose considering the state he was in.

As we ran as fast as we could through his neighbour's gardens, I noticed Steve was starting to veer slightly to the right, which I assumed was due to his inebriated state this was surely going to work to my advantage because I had chosen the most direct route, and was now a dead cert to win 'The Frampton Cotterell Grand National'

As I jumped the penultimate fence with victory assured, I noticed something glistening on the ground below me... 'you bastard!' I shouted as I plunged almost head first into his neighbours ill-kept fish pond.

Steve stood there laughing, as I splashed around trying to get a foot hold in a very slippery, dirty, smelly pond, bade me good night and left me to a very cold, wet and somewhat defeated walk home.

Band night at the Locarno was almost always packed out, with Scooters parked outside, and a mass of green parkas everywhere, for a few hours we would all be in mod heaven, especially as it was one of the few times we were actually allowed in with our white socks on. I was lucky enough to see many mod revival bands there, especially Secret Affair, The Beat, Dexys Midnight Runners, Madness, The Specials, and the most anticipated of all The Jam.

The ground floor had a rather plush cinema complex which could easily seat around 850 people and this is where we watched *Quadrophenia* many times during its first release. Predictably there was always a lot of excitement and noisy chattering before the film started, especially on one occasion when a rumour started to circulate that a few of the *Quadrophenia* cast had turned up for the film's premier in punk-style clothing. How could this be? Surely they weren't punks? Our heroes punks? Never...

The whole place was usually crammed wall-to-wall with parka-wearing mods, an irony not totally lost on the audience, which usually resulted in the auditorium being filled with laughter, when Phil Daniels recited the immortal lines...

'I don't wanna be the same as everybody else.'

'That's why I'm a mod, see?'

'I mean, you gotta be somebody, ain't you?'

As the lights dimmed we would sit almost motionless, eagerly anticipating the main feature. Before *Quadrophenia* started there would usually be some amusing Silk Cut cigarette adverts or scaremongering political party broadcasts comparing the Labour Government to the Marx

Brothers, and if we were lucky the earlier released motion picture *Scum* featuring several of the *Quadrophenia* cast. I also remember seeing a documentary about the London mod scene featuring Secret Affair and The Chords, which was always guaranteed to ramp up the excitement before the forthcoming film, not just any film, this was 'our' film… *Quadrophenia*.

  Having seen the film so many times over the years it's hard to be impartial about it, yes it has its flaws and historical errors but it's gone on to be one of the most revered British youth films ever produced. I think it's best to accept it as a very good piece of British cinema and just sit back and enjoy it.

  With the release of *Quadrophenia* in the cinemas and its positive reception across the country, mod as a youth culture seemed to be everywhere. The media weren't slow to pick up on the film's success, producing TV programmes and newspaper special editions to satisfy what seemed like an insatiable interest in all things mod.

  Looking back I suppose it was inevitable that someone somewhere was going to dive into the crowd below just like 'Jimmy' had done in the Brighton Nightclub scene. So it wasn't much of a surprise when one night a figure similar to a well-suited Phil Daniels was seen climbing onto the Locarno's balcony rail. As the startled house band ground to a halt, all eyes turned upwards to see the 'Jimmy wannabe' still grooving to the by now nonexistent music. He seized his moment as the bouncers clumsily grabbed for him, and gracefully launched himself in the air like some majestic bird over the Pacific Ocean. Sadly, for him this wasn't Brighton, or a film set and the Bristol Locarno crowd thought it was more prudent to step out of the way rather than break the fall of the night's unexpected 'show stopper'. For a brief moment, all went quiet, until there was a rather nasty splatting sound as he hit the hard wooden dance floor with his head. Moments later four rather burly bouncers came to his aid with no compassion at all, quickly carrying him out of the main hall, completely ignoring his protestations that his 'head hurt' as they bundled him unsympathetically out of the front door dropping him once again onto the cold unforgiving floor.

  Not wanting an evening in town to end, we would usually head for the Gloucester Road, one of the main arteries leading out of Bristol. Gloucester Road in the early hours was like a very poor man's version of the Las Vegas strip, filled with drunken revellers milling around and several popular fast food outlets that never seemed to close. Of these the Southern Fried Chicken bar and Schwartz Bros burger bar were by far the most popular, serving fast food that at 2am in the morning tasted like it had come from some of the finest restaurants in London.

  For those that had managed to avoid the mayhem that was regularly unleashed across the city centre in the early hours the journey home could be just as eventful and at times very dangerous, as the streets were still alive with many gangs wanting to do some sort of damage to anyone that crossed their path.

On one occasion, as our car weaved unsteadily up Gloucester Road, it became apparent that the slow-moving vehicle in front of us was a police patrol car. Trying not to attract too much attention by suddenly driving over cautiously we were delighted to see four skinheads laying the boot into a punk rocker just ahead in the middle of the road, delighted that is because this would surely divert any attention away from us. Expecting a sudden stop we dropped back as the police car slowed to a gradual halt with a surprising lack of urgency.

Sitting there watching the skinheads kicking their victim, we were amazed that they seemed completely oblivious to the police car's presence. The kicking frenzy eventually came to an abrupt end when one of the skinheads realised they had an uninvited audience watching their every vicious move, then they took off into the night, in four different directions, lessening the chance of being arrested. It was surely time for the dramatic car door opening and Starsky & Hutch style chase to ensue, after all this was pretty violent stuff and the police had every reason to intervene, although somewhat belatedly.

I'm not sure what sort of discussion must have been going on inside the police car, but whatever the conclusion it certainly wasn't the one we expected. As the skinheads disappeared, so did the police car albeit somewhat slower than the skinheads who must have been home and tucked up safely in their beds before the police decided to take any sort of affirmative action. Which in this case was a very decisive slow navigation around the punk's prone body, followed by a very leisurely drive up Gloucester Road as if nothing unusual had happened. Just another normal day's vigilant work patrolling the streets of the city, by Bristol's finest.

No doubt lessons were learned…

If we weren't spending our time at the New Bristol Centre then we would usually be found in the Wheatsheaf public house on Winterbourne High Street, which had been our 'local' since 1976, and for some reason, one of the only pubs in the area we hadn't managed to get banned from during our 'mildly anarchistic' punk period.

The Wheatsheaf was a very busy pub used by predominantly young customers, due to its proximity to the school a few hundred metres up the road. Very rarely was there any trouble, except for the odd disagreement about someone cheating at cards or whose turn it was to buy the drinks.

The Wheatsheaf had managed to remain a quite uneventful pub for the times, only once getting its name in the local papers, when fellow school friend Kevin Norton was attacked by a group of iron bar wielding masked men. Completely unprovoked, the gang had arrived with the sole purpose of causing someone grievous bodily harm; 'tooled up' they set about him with iron bars, guaranteeing him a hospital bed.

Most of the time the pub was a vibrant popular place, especially when they installed what was then a cutting-edge very addictive space invaders machine.

Compared to today's computer games, it was rather basic. But back in 1979 this was state-of-the-art stuff; row upon row of little aliens would descend from a space ship in the hope that they would reach terra firma, long before you could finish them off with a single-shot space gun. On paper this would seem a rather balanced conflict, except for the fact that these cunning aliens had the advantage of dropping bombs on you and speeding up just as you thought you had got the better of them.

The space invader machine was situated near the rear entrance door that led into the car park. Anyone entering the pub would have to walk past the machine usually surrounded by addicted, amateur space cadets. One fateful evening as myself and a few others stood around waiting our turn, the door opened and three strikingly well-dressed young men walked in. These guys had obviously spent a lot of money getting their 1960s look just right. It wasn't so much that they had a mod look about them, but more a Beatles look, which made them stand out even more. With their made-to-measure grey, shiny suits sporting velvet collars, crisp white button-down shirts and cuban-heeled black leather boots they made their way confidently to the bar, with all eyes upon them. Some looked at them with admiration, others with inquisitive interest, and some, it would soon transpire, with complete jealousy.

Sadly, a few in the pub fell into the latter category. One of them, Steve, moved very quickly towards the bar with no other intention than to intimidate the newcomers. After a while it became very clear that things were going to take a turn for the worse when Steve became very vocal about the fact that one of his loafer shoes had been accidentally trodden on by one of our unwelcome guests.

"Mike, Mike... did you see that?"

"See what?" I replied.

"He stood on my loafer!"

"Well, so what?"

"But it's my new loafer!" he exclaimed.

"So?" I replied, pretending to be mystified.

In utter disbelief I watched as he returned to the bar, with Dave in tow. Disappointed, I assume that I hadn't shared his anger that someone had accidentally stepped on his shoe.

Sensing that things were going to very quickly turn ugly, I went to the bar, positioning myself so that I could see what was happening. Within moments of ordering my drink, I heard a loud smash as a glass was knocked over. Suddenly all hell broke loose, reminiscent of a Wild West bar fight; tables went flying, punches were thrown, and glasses were smashed. These guys obviously knew how to handle themselves and very quickly had got the better of Steve and Dave, who had obviously bitten off more than they could chew in trying to teach them a lesson for accidentally stepping on Steve's prized brown loafer. As I was standing behind them, I managed to get the better of one of them and pinned him to the floor. Whilst holding him down, I shouted over to Nick who was sitting on a stool, still playing the space invader machine whilst all around him, utter chaos and disorder reigned.

"Nick! Nick! Give us a hand!"

"Hang on, hang on," he quickly replied.

"Nick we need your help!"

"I can't, I can't,"

"For God's sake, why not?" I shouted.

"I'm on for the high score!" He replied.

"Fair comment," I thought. "You can't argue with that reasoning."

Within minutes it was all over, and the three of them left, leaving us with an ominous warning, "We will be back."

Dave had been head-butted and was taken upstairs by the landlady for treatment. In the meantime people were mostly standing around in shock as to what had happened. One of the locals came over to me with a worried look on his face. "You've done it now," he said.

"Why's that?" I asked.

"They were from the Trident pub in Downend."

"And your point is?" I queried.

"It's a hard pub. They won't forget, and they will be back."

From then on my main thoughts were of getting out

of there as soon as possible, but with Dave upstairs being nursed, time was quickly ticking away.

Eventually Dave came downstairs and we quickly made our way out of the pub. As I opened the front door leading onto the High Street, I saw five cars pulling up with all their doors open. Just as I turned back into the pub I heard a voice.

"Hey you! We've got something nice for you here." That one remark still to this day sends a chill down my spine.

Back in the pub everyone was unsure about what to do. As I did a quick mental check that everyone was present, I noticed that Dave wasn't in the bar. "Where's Dave?" I shouted.

"He went out the back way to his car," someone replied. "I think he's still out there".

I turned to everyone in the bar and motioned to them, "Come on. Let's go and get him." And charged out of the door.

Normally in these circumstances you would hope that at least two or three people would follow you out, and on this occasion I'd like to say that I was pleasantly surprised by the overwhelming support I got. Albeit a fool's errand, but alas dear reader it wasn't to be. As I ran down the path to where Dave had parked, I noticed a certain lack of company. As I stood there completely alone, before me was Dave's car with every light and window smashed in, even the sunroof, and Dave cowering inside as the 'Trident Twenty' tried to extricate him. My sudden appearance drew their attention, and if any one of you has ever seen the film *Starship Troopers* then you should be able to visualise what it was like, as they all streamed off the car towards me like homicidal alien bugs.

This wasn't really my finest hour. Not because of the situation I now found myself in, but in answering the question that was soon to follow. As they encircled me, I really wanted to appear brave but courage has a time and place and this was neither. I could see the steam from their breath mixed with the undeniable smell of alcohol rising into the cold night sky. Most of them were dressed quite normally, but the ringleader was a skinhead; just a bit taller than myself, with a swagger and demeanour that only the confidence of numbers can give you. He was the first to approach me. "It's nothing to do with me," I blurted. "I'm not even from around here."

"Yeah? So where are you from then?" the skinhead sarcastically enquired with a breath that toothpaste couldn't cure.

I suspect at this point I might have had a 50/50 chance of getting out of the rather tricky situation I now found myself in, although I do appreciate that these guys were after blood, and mine had just been handed to them on a plate. But there was always the hope that a good reply might get me off the hook.

For a moment my mind went completely blank and I blurted out the one place uppermost in my mind, "Downend?"

The last thing I remember seeing, besides a sixteen-hole Dr Marten boot smashing into my head, were the ambulance doors closing.

  Frenchay Hospital Head Injury Ward, was to be my new home for the time being, and to my utter surprise and delight I found that Doug had been admitted to another ward close by, after sustaining double vision when one of the 'Trident Twenty' caught him off guard and hit him with a baseball bat around the head. Very soon we became quite institutionalised. I remember one particular sunny afternoon outside the ward recuperating with nothing left to discuss except what we had been served for lunch, when we realised that we had both eaten the same meal, although alarmingly it was called something quite different depending on which ward you were on.

  In those days counselling wasn't something that was really forthcoming, and it was very much a time of stiff upper lip and get on with it. Now looking back I can see that the whole event had a huge psychological effect on me, one that still reverberates to this day.

  I spent the next few months looking over my shoulder in complete fear of reprisals, especially as someone had daubed 'We will be back' in 12-inch high letters on the Wheatsheaf's exterior wall.

  The court case went well and all those involved were prosecuted, although strangely I wasn't invited to give evisence, which at the time suited me just fine as I didn't really want to see my attackers again.

  As time passed the harrowing memory and flashbacks of that senseless awful night faded as life carried on pretty much as it had done before, with one exception, for a while I started getting into fights quite regularly, usually with little or no provocation; for obvious reasons I wanted to take on the world, a world that had dealt me quite vicious injuries, and so I went about venting my anger on anyone that stood in my way.

If there was a funny side to all this it was the fact that my head was so heavily bandaged that after they were removed, my hair stuck straight upwards like a toilet brush, even after being washed several times. For weeks I had to go everywhere with my parka hood up as I looked liked I was in a permanent state of 'hair raising' shock.

Girls hadn't really been on my radar for some time, although I'd done quite well during my school years; becoming a punk didn't really enamour me to the opposite sex. Looking back I must have had a few fallow years as my most vivid recollection of any female company was the night I lost my virginity at the age of 16 to a lovely girl called Linda.

Linda had been in the same year as me at school and after a while we become an item with her half heartedly running away from home, and staying out way past her bed time on quite a few occasions. Of course it was all my fault from her parents' point of view, and I suppose it was in some respect, not that I encouraged her, but we did enjoy each other's company, and time does fly by when you're having fun... even if it is freezing cold whilst fumbling through each other's clothing behind the newsagents.

Most of our dates involved cold open spaces or obscured doorways, as at 16 there aren't really many places you can go. So when she gave me the opportunity to join her babysitting one evening, I was more than happy to oblige. I remember turning up on my Yamaha FS1E DX moped at the appointed time, sporting my best clothes and underwear with an air of confidence that I hoped would hide my sheer terror. Tucked under my arm was the one album I was sure would get her into the mood for romance... was it David Cassidy? No... Then maybe Donny Osmond? No... Surely not Slade... Hardly. In my infinite wisdom I took along the Please Please Me album by The Beatles... not realising at the time the complete irony of it all.

It was one of those evenings that you hoped something was going to happen, but nervously would try and skirt around any sort of reference to it. As I played the game of innuendo and double entendre, she politely smiled and nodded at me knowingly, although to be honest I suspect in reality as soon as I turned my back she was rolling her rather pretty eyes in bemusement.

As the evening moved on it seemed like we were both involved in a psychological war of attrition, but one I was determined to win. As the wine flowed and we both got that rather warm feeling inside, I managed to get to what has commonly become known as first base.

If only I had heeded my old sports masters advice. 'Michael it's a marathon not a sprint' because in my haste and inexperience I managed to get to fourth base in well under 20 seconds, completely missing out second and third.

Oh how I wish I could say all was romance, with the sound of The Beatles singing 'Love Me Do' or at least 'Baby it's You', but no, the irony gods were working overtime that evening as the words I still remember ringing in my ears at the very moment I lost my virginity were 'Please please me whoa yea, like I please you', words I suspect more befitting Linda's situation than my own.

Without going into too much detail, I'd heard that a girl couldn't get pregnant if she sat in a freezing cold bath. So up the stairs she went, equally as panic stricken as myself and keen to try anything that might lessen the chance of an unwanted teenage pregnancy. As I sat motionless by the nice warm open fire, I could hear the unmistakable sounds of her getting into a very cold bath. More concerned with my own plight I sat their motionless weighing up the chances of me actually becoming a father at my very first, misguided attempt. Sometime later she came back down stairs wrapped in a very thin towel, almost blue with her teeth chattering in a way I've never seen or heard since. It's a wonder she didn't catch pneumonia, but she took it all in good spirits and didn't seem too surprised when in true gentlemanly style I made my feeble excuses and quickly left.

In 1979 my fallow period was about to abruptly end, when I was lucky enough to start seeing Jenny on a regular basis. Jenny was also a former pupil of the Ridings and was certainly a feather in anyone's cap that was lucky enough to date her. She sort of chose me which was nice as in reality she could have chosen any partner she wanted. Jenny had dated the older boys from school and was way ahead in the experience game, I can only describe her experience in one way... she knew things... make of that, what you will.

I didn't really treat Jenny with the respect she deserved; I was young and had discovered the excitement of being part of a gang where my mates came first and my girlfriend second. I can't remember once taking her into Bristol with me or anywhere else for that matter except the local pub. I'd make my way back from Steamers Nightclub in Bristol at some ungodly hour, arrive at her mother's house and throw pebbles at her bedroom window until she would come down and let me in. This went on for several months until the novelty wore off.

I do remember our relationship ended not long after I was cordially invited to tea at Jen's grandmother's home on Winterbourne High Street. Not sure if this was to be a 'prospective family member' interview or merely a social gathering, I erred on the side of caution and decided to make the best impression I could. Without going too far over the top I dug out a nice white shirt, my favourite three-button jacket, sta pressed trousers, and cuban-heeled winkle picker boots I had been loathed to discard from my punk days, and the only aftershave I had ever owned, a very large glass bottle of Faberge Brut; as per Henry Cooper's instructions I 'splashed it all over'.

As we walked hand in hand on that lovely summer's evening the world seemed a wonderful place, slightly marred by Jen's nausea that was brought on she suspected by my overzealous use of aftershave.

Her grandmother was most welcoming as we entered her small but cosy one-bedroom flat. It was obvious she took great pride and joy in her home as she led us proudly through the small spotless hallway along the nicely carpeted corridor and into a very much lived in but immaculate front room, where she had kindly laid on tea and biscuits and if I remember correctly a small plate of finely cut cucumber sandwiches.

As the small talk unfolded I took great care in complimenting her on her lovely home and how everything seemed well... just perfect. I was certain I was doing rather well in the impress the grandmother stakes. With a touch of laughter here and a smile there the air was filled with conviviality; the conversation floated along at a lively pace, interrupted only occasionally by a very odd nasal twitch Jen's grandmother had cultivated since I had moved the rather comfy chair I was sitting in nearer the electric fire.

Everything seemed to be going admirably, until that is the conversation took an unexpected turn.

"Do you smell something?" She asked sniffing and twitching her nose.

Jen and I looked at each other wondering what her grandmother was referring too.

"No?" we replied shaking our heads as our eyes conferred across the room.

With a flash of inspiration, I recalled the amount of Brut I had liberally 'splashed all over' earlier.

Leaning forward I smiled a knowing smile and offered what I was sure was the answer to her unexpected question.

"Oh, that's my Brut aftershave, rather overpowering but rather intoxicating I'm sure you would agree?"

My confidence was starting to grow because the evening was going much better than I could have hoped and my liberal use of the Brut was obviously starting to work its advertised magic. Henry Cooper, Barry Sheene and Kevin Keegan I assured myself would all be very proud of me.

"That's shit!" she proclaimed.

"Sorry?" I muttered as my eyes darted across to Jen's in the hope she would save me from whatever was coming next.

As If no one had heard her the first time Jen's grandmother repeated her outburst.

"That's shit!"

Slumping back in the now not-so-comfy chair, I sat mortified as I felt my confidence and colour very quickly drain from my body.

Staring directly into my eyes for longer than was comfortable, she slowly lowered her gaze down the length of my body coming to an abrupt halt at one of my feet.

"There!" she proclaimed pointing at my rather or so I thought shiny winkle picker boots.

"There!" she reiterated in a much louder tone than I thought such a small-framed woman could possibly muster.

Looking to Jen for help, I noticed that her complexion had also changed, from the rosy, red-cheeked look she often sported to a deathly white one, the likes of which I had never seen grace her face before. She, just like her grandmother also seemed rather fascinated by my feet, underlined by a quick bout of surreptitious nodding.

Looking down, all I could think was 'oh shit', and quite rightly so, as there stuck to one of my boots was the remains of what had been a very proud moment I'm sure for the rather large dog that had produced it, the rest unfortunately was evenly dispersed throughout Jen's grandmother's pride and joy. I had literally, not for the first or last time managed to get myself 'in the shit'.

I closed the door on the way out.

Chapter 5

SCOOTERS AT THE JOLLY COBBLER

By mid 1980, having moved out of Doug's house under a bit of a cloud, I found myself living in Yate, several miles up the road from leafy Frampton Cotterell. I'm not exactly sure how it happened, but somehow I had managed to convince my older sister Barbara and her husband Keith what they really needed to complete their matrimonial bliss was a lodger, or to be more exact me. Keith was a lovely man, although most of the time he seemed to be completely oblivious that there was anyone else living in the house except him and my sister.

I suppose now in hindsight it's understandable that my new brother-in-law, was rather crestfallen when my sister announced that her favourite brother (her only one) was moving in, with no firm plan to actually move out anytime soon. After all, I hadn't really enamoured myself to him, when I read that the very day they were to be married, The Beatles *Rock 'n' Roll* album was to hit the shops and given the choice, I plumped to spend the day travelling into Bristol to get 74 minutes of vinyl heaven, rather than see my sister wed. So not surprising when all considered he carried on as much as possible pretending that there wasn't any more than two people living in his house, neither of which was me.

For hours I would keep out the way by sitting in

my sparsely furnished cold bedroom, (something I could never work out because the rest of the house seemed reasonably warm although I know suspect this was part of Keith's devious plan to get rid of me) playing my prized collection of vinyl records from my personal favourites such as The Jam, Nine Below Zero, Secret Affair, The Specials, The Action and of course the Mods Mayday album that really seemed to captured the energy and excitement of what was happening at the time.

Young Vespa Vince Ayres who lived just around the corner, would to my annoyance frequently turn up on his 50cc Vespa scooter demanding I should listen to some obscure northern soul records he had discovered in a second-hand shop or other. Northern soul meant absolutely nothing to me and for years just sounded like a lot of failed or knock off Tamla Motown records. I was completely oblivious to Wigan Casino, all-nighters or for that matter cared. I had my favourites and that was the way it was going to stay, or so I thought...

The revival bands were going from strength especially Madness and The Jam. But with the release the 1980s album Ultimate Action my musical tastes started to broaden. The Action were one of those bands that everyone seems to agree should have made it, well everyone it would seem except the 1960s record-buying public. With Reg King's dulcet soulful voice the group would release single after single that just didn't seem to catch the public's imagination. This album alone paved the way for my greater interest in original more obscure mod music, reaching way beyond the revival.

Yate at times wasn't for the faint hearted, although during the day it could appear quite pleasant, with its suburban layout and communal spaces, at night it could turn quite violent. The Four Seasons pub near the main shopping centre was renowned for its pool table, sadly not in any way connected to sport, but for the use of its cues across people's heads. No one was safe, and so I tended to avoid most of the pubs, as they were frequented by many locals that didn't take kindly to outsiders, even if they knew them.

Although quite a large town, mods in Yate were in very short supply, at most I can only think of about seven that regularly met up. Being in the minority we would all stick together as much as possible, preferring the long regular trips into Bristol rather than tempt fate visiting a Yate pub and ending up at the end of a cue.

Kingswood was to almost become my second home, after my friend Colin Musty suggested we visit the well known Bristol City pub, The Jolly Cobbler one warm summer's evening in early 1980. The inside of the 'Cobbler' was regularly frequented by a vast array of football supporters and long-haired leather-jacketed biker types, who had never as far as I knew owned any form of two-wheeled transport, but would probably spend most of their time watching Easy Rider on VHS, getting high and listening to their well-worn copy of Saxon's *Wheels of Steel.*

The outside, on the other hand, was the meeting place of a disparate group of teenagers that just went by the name of The Cobbler Lot; a collection of friendly, fun, mods, that wanted nothing more than to have a good time and ride their scooters.

As we pulled up that evening, we were met with great suspicion by the likes of Geoff Rice, Andy Baker, Piggy and Phil Henley. Although Andy seemed to be the 'leader', if there was such a thing, it was probably more due to his height and air of confidence than any superior show of outer strength.

This initial meeting was to form friendships that I still value to this day.

Piggy was by no means as overweight as his nickname would imply, but at the time he seemed to cast a much larger shadow than the rest of us, and with short cropped hair, Union Jack T-shirt, MA1 Flight Jacket and Dr Marten boots, he resembled more of a skinhead than any of the mods he had chosen to hang around with. Having someone of Piggy's stature around was always helpful when trouble came calling.

I remember one summer's day when Piggy abruptly ended his highly competitive game of darts, when a shout went out, that two skinheads were approaching the Jolly Cobbler on trials bikes. Piggy was literally a one man stampede as he careered out of the pub brushing all in his path aside, favourite darts in hand, which he proceeded to let fly at the now totally terrified skinheads. One of the darts scored a direct hit and stuck in the back of one of them as they turned tail and set off as fast as they could in the same direction they had come from. I can still see Piggy now vainly chasing them down the road, protesting and gesticulating at the loss of his dart and demanding its return.

Geoff Rice was slightly younger than me and was in a word 'fun', and had spent his whole life in the pursuit of it. Being around Geoff was always filled with an uncertainty as you never knew what trouble he would get into next, or which A&E Department or police cell you would have to go and visit him in. Although Geoff's sense of fun could at times cause each and every one of us inconvenience, it was a small price to pay for the knowledge that if there was any trouble, Geoff would either guard your back, or stand shoulder to shoulder with you until he was the last man standing.

Chapter 6

ON THE ROAD

Most evenings would be spent riding our scooters around the back streets of Bristol, visiting friends or hanging around The Cobbler enjoying the fun of being part of a gang, and having mates that shared your idea of what having a good time really was.

When we did go on a ride, seaside destinations always held a particular attraction, so on one particular evening about 15 of us decided to travel to the seaside town of Clevedon, some 20 miles west of Bristol, to have a cup of coffee, cigarettes and something to eat. Although this sounds a complete waste of time, we did it for the sheer enjoyment of riding our scooters together, with the added bonus that something might happen. At the arranged time we set off from The Cobbler through roads that we knew were fairly safe until we got into the centre of Bristol. Once we got through to the other side of the city, we could drop our guard slightly as we ventured through the villages along the route.

Sometimes the locals could get quite irate when they realised that a bunch of scooter-riding mods had the audacity to ride through 'their' village without notifying them or seeking their permission, thus denying them the opportunity of throwing the odd beer glass or brick at their unannounced guests as they quickly passed through.

The more territorial locals would occasionally

chase us in their cars, until they realised that they were actually confronting a bunch of people that had more experience of road rage than they could ever imagine, and that they would probably come off much worse if it actually came to blows.

  Clevedon always seemed to be a very grey sleepy town, quiet, uneventful, that hadn't changed much in the previous 100 years. With its old Victorian buildings pensioners and dilapidated pier, it was one of the few places on earth that you felt Agatha Christie's Miss Marple or Hercule Poirot could probably visit and not come across a single murdered body.

  As we arrived, Clevedon appeared even more sleepy than usual, especially around the estuary wall near the pier where we usually parked up our scooters to have the requisite John Player Blue or Lambert & Butler cigarette, discuss the journey down, and compare the attributes of each scooter's saddle (which was quite common after a fairly long journey). After a while we would make our way to the local coffee bar before the journey back to Bristol.

  As we pulled up outside, we all glanced at each other to signify that we had noticed the presence of a Hell's Angel type motorbike in the car park. This was unusual because we had never come across any trouble in Clevedon before or knew of any bikers that used the coffee bar. There was always the chance more might arrive, but we decided to stand our ground and carry on in, wary of anything that might be coming our way.

In the corner sat the bike's rider, an ugly looking, greasy haired, leather-clad 20 something, pretending not to notice our arrival. As we eyed him up one of our party realised they knew him from old, and reassured us he was harmless, and wouldn't cause any trouble. As the evening wore on a few of us approached him and struck up a conversation, which almost restored our faith in bikers, and that, not all of them wanted to kill us, or at least cause us some form of grievous bodily harm. All seemed quite friendly and convivial as we joked among ourselves and the biker until it was time to leave.

The journey home was usually different to the journey down, as most of us came from different parts of Bristol and so we would split up and take different routes. This wasn't always the best scenario as there was safety in numbers, but usually late in the evening you could get around quite unnoticed unless a car decided to push you into a ditch or a biker tried to kick you off.

As we all said our goodbyes, we headed off in single file towards the town centre, completely oblivious of the mayhem that was going on behind. Unbeknownst to us, the ugly, greasy biker had slowly worked his way along our line, lashing out with his boot as he passed each unsuspecting scooter, managing to catch several completely off guard. As we started to pull over he realised the game was up and sped off confident he had got away with it. Leaving a pile of damaged scooters and bodies in his wake.

PUNKS ON SCOOTERS

He must have felt really proud of himself having convinced us of his love of all things two-wheeled and his ambivalence to the old mods and rockers rivalry. Even those that had been more wary of him were eventually duped by his fond farewells as we had left the coffee bar.

Pretty proud that is until his bike came to an abrupt halt as it smashed head first into an oncoming car as he went around the corner, catapulting him some 10 feet in the air, over the car with arms and legs flailing like somebody that had jumped out of an aeroplane and just realised he had forgotten to pack his parachute.

I'd like to think that each and every one one of us had some degree of a sympathetic nature, but on this occasion we all carried on our way leaving him where he had landed, completely happy that the biker had got his just deserts, although a few of us did give him a farewell wave and smile as he writhed in pain on the nice hard tarmac road.

Venturing out on the scooter was usually fraught with some sort of danger. If you were lucky enough to avoid the Capri-driving motorist who would try to knock you off for the sheer fun of it then you could usually fall victim to the incessant badgering by the local police force, hoping to prosecute you for some spurious infringement of the law.

I paint a rather negative picture of the police and at times I'm probably being slightly unfair, but as many scooter-riding friends of the period would attest, they could sometimes be absolute bastards.

Recreational drugs although easily available have never really been my thing, except for cigarettes and alcohol. A 'stop and search' by the local constabulary could be a regular occurrence especially if you were travelling home on your scooter in the early hours of the morning and weaving quite uncontrollably from one side of the road to the other. On one occasion I hadn't noticed the vehicle behind me which I suppose goes to confirm the sort of state I was in, especially when you consider how many rear view mirrors I had fitted to my scooter. With a screech of rubber on tarmac a police patrol car swerved in front of me almost knocking me off. The door of the car swung open and out stepped a very smug looking police officer.

"You've had a good evening I see," he said in a terse sarcastic tone.

Before I had time to think of something witty to say he quickly followed with some quite tricky questions or so I thought...

"Where have you been then sonny? On our way back from Brighton are we?"

"Ummm no, I'm just on my way home from a night club... Lourdes," I replied.

"Oh they've got nightclubs in France now have they; you're quite the little jet setter aren't you?"

"No not the Lourdes in France the one in Fairfax Street the night club, do you know it?" I asked hoping to strike up some sort of amiable conversation.

"You trying to be funny lad?"

"No, no Officer not at all, just trying to answer your

questions."

"That's good then, we wouldn't want to upset an officer of Her Majesty's Government now would we?"

Before I had a chance to answer, he brushed past me and started looking over my scooter.

"What's this then? Some sort of sewing machine?"

"It's a scooter... Lambretta... 125cc," I replied.

"A Lambretta eh, where's the side panels then?"

Luckily for me just before I had a chance to tell him the Colditz rabbit had them, he interjected...

"You got a license and insurance for that thing then?"

"Yes, yes, I think I've got it here somewhere."

I fumbled in my pockets emptying all I was carrying onto my scooter seat. Cigarettes, matches, loose change, tin foil wrap, wallet.

"What's that?" he demanded pointing at the small pile in front of him, "that tin foil thing?"

"It's my pills," I chokingly replied looking at him quite meekly.

For the first time I saw him smile.

"Pills is it? You're a regular little box of surprises aren't you... open it up."

Nervously I fumbled with the tin foil wrap to reveal two small white tablets.

"Give them to me." he demanded.

His eyes seemed to grow larger with excitement, like a child receiving a much desired toy, as I handed over the crumpled foil wrap.

His eyes slowly narrowed as the excitement

drained from his face to a look of disappointment as he read the imprint on the tablets... Aspirin.

He rapidly lost interest in me after checking my licence and insurance and left me with the parting words I shall never forget.

"Now, fuck off home Michael, because you'd never pass the breathalyser in the state you're in. Go on fuck off."

These were very different times indeed.

Every corner turned had its possible challenges. Certain places were known as 'no-go' areas and if you did enter them you would try to get through, as quickly as possible, usually under the cover of darkness. I've seen pubs almost completely empty out, as I've driven past, to be greeted with a hail of glasses smashing on the road all around me. At times like these there were only two things you could do, accelerate as fast as possible and pray, to any god that came to mind, that your engine wouldn't stall.

Any trouble from motorcyclists, or jitters as we called them, was usually from the 250 boys, young wannabe Hell's Angels legally riding bikes up to 250cc on a provisional licence. These 'bikers' would either try to kick you off or lash out at you with some kind of weapon as they went past, bravely speeding up, in the knowledge that with their superior engine power you wouldn't be able to confront them face to face.

Surprisingly, the more hardened bikers didn't seem to have any interest in us at all. I remember a few of us returning one Sunday afternoon from a scooter run in Torquay, when in the distance I saw a cloud of exhaust fumes slowly moving towards us. As the smoke got nearer I could vaguely see some thirty-odd, very hard looking, middle-aged Hell's Angels coming towards us. I knowingly turned to my mate that was sat on the pillion and said, "We are dead..."

Quickly we all pulled over, not really knowing what to do except hopefully put up some semblance of a fight before coming to the inevitable rather sticky end. Tool box doors were opened in the desperate search for anything that could be used as an effective weapon, spanners, adjustable wrenches or hammers were always popular as these could usually be explained away to the police when pulled for a stop and search. My personal weapon of choice was the crash helmet which could pack quite a blow if swung correctly, flattening the intended victim if you managed to catch them on the side of the head.

As we all stood by the side of the road pitifully 'tooled up' compared to what the Hells Angels were rumoured to carry, shaking more in fear than anger or aggression only to see the Hell's Angels slowly ride past, looking straight ahead as if we weren't there. Now I know this sounds kind of strange, but in some way for us this was worse than the inevitable 'good hiding' we were expecting, as it was as though we weren't even worth acknowledging, let alone killing.

Long distance trips outside Bristol were called scooter runs or just runs; usually to a coastal town of some sort, most probably in recognition of the heady days of the mods and rocker clashes of the 1960s.

On a good day, some 30 scooters would convene at either The Black Swan on Stapleton Road, The Jolly Cobbler in Kingswood or Steamers night club on Prince Street, most would usually arrive completely unprepared, devoid of any money, sleeping bags or spare clothes.

On most occasions the smaller scooters would take the lead, with the rest following closely behind, holding up all the traffic, as the large convoy pottered along at 30mph, much to the annoyance of all the car drivers and their passengers. On a few occasions I can remember being stopped by the police and threatened with arrest, after someone had reported us for purposely going too slowly and causing traffic delays.

After several hours, with various stops along the way for a cigarette break, a police spot check or break downs, we would arrive at our destination completely shattered, but excited and relieved that we had all managed to make it in one piece. Those that could afford it would book into a bed & breakfast, whilst the majority that couldn't, would sleep rough, usually in a car park or empty garage.

The night air would be filled with the sound and smell of two-stroke engines as more and more scooters arrived from all over the country. Stories new and old would be shared, accompanied by the endless consumption of cider and cigarettes way into the early hours of the morning. It was a bonding experience that in some cases would last a lifetime. The rising of the sun would signal the time to search out some greasy café prepared to serve a ramshackle pack of scooterists bacon, eggs and beans, and a very welcome warm mug of tea or coffee, followed by a dessert of the aforementioned John Player Blue or Lambert & Butler cigarette.

The afternoon would be filled with drinking, catching up with old friends from various parts of the country, and endless rumours that something more interesting was happening somewhere else. By the evening, the pubs would be filled with as many as 3000 scooterists all in various states of getting drunk, with only the odd serious incident which could involve someone either getting glassed or on a rare occasion getting stabbed.

After a quick wash and brush up in the local public toilets, the day was usually spent roaming the streets like any other tourists with the added expectation that trouble could 'kick off' at any time. It wasn't always the skinheads or bikers that would arrive looking for trouble; often it was the local constabulary. With their heavy-handed approach they would sit menacingly inside their riot vans, just itching to start some sort of confrontation to warrant their overtime pay, and get their names in the papers, just as their counterparts had done in Clacton and Margate in the 1960s.

This is exactly what the police did during the Weston-super-Mare scooter rally I attended in 1980. Riot vans full of police were positioned for no other reason than to intimidate the scooterists that had gathered in the many bars and cafes along the sea front. When a beer glass was thrown at one of the riot vans all hell broke loose as the police seized the opportunity to baton charge the many scooterists drinking and chatting outside.

 Myself and a few others had been talking to one of the friendlier skinheads who went by the name of Plebby who was easily identifiable because in his infinite wisdom he had felt the need to have Made In Bristol permanently tattooed across his forehead. Most people would have thought a birth certificate more than adequate proof of where you were born. Within seconds he was unconscious on the floor as one of the out-of-control charging local constabulary smashed their baton down on his skull causing him to collapse in a heap right in front of us.

 Stepping over him the police continued to move forward using their riot shields to contain us by forcing us up against the building wall. The attack on Plebby was vicious and completely unprovoked as he had his back to his attacker. The police force used excessive violence to contain a crowd that was doing nothing more than exercising their right to congregate in a public place. These were violent times but the police on many occasions were the problem not the solution. Some 30 years later there is still debate on how to deal with crowds and how the use of sirens, flashing lights and intimidating tactics can cause the problem they are purportedly supposed to prevent.

I never saw Plebby again and can only assume he was all right as I never heard anything to the contrary. But if I did see him, I'm sure I would recognise him especially as 'Made In Bristol' would be written all over his face… literally.

Torquay Scooter Rally did get quite heated one August Bank Holiday, when the police called in the helicopters it seemed that things were starting to get out of hand, I suggested it was probably time we left, and so Vince, Tim and myself headed home long before any of the others we had travelled down with.

As we rode through Broadclyst we were surprised to see some 30 odd bloodthirsty members of The Satan's Slaves motorcycle gang, lying in wait for us. The Satan's Slaves' Devon Chapter, so we found out later were based just up the road in Exeter and weren't to be tangled with. As we passed, they just stood and stared at us rather menacingly. It was obvious they were looking for trouble, as in their hands it was easy to spot the, chains, baseball bats and iron bars.

We put as much distance between them and ourselves as we possibly could. After a while breathing a sigh of relief, we all thought we had got away with it, only to realise the road had been blocked ahead of us, and we had ridden into a well-planned trap. As pandemonium broke out around us the tourists sat stationary in their cars in utter disbelief, watching as The Satan's Slaves attacked us from all directions. It was as if we were in a scene from the film *The Warriors*, we had obviously crossed the Satan's Slaves territory, and they didn't like it, one little bit. Luckily no one was seriously hurt especially when you consider the weapons they were carrying. I later heard that Vince had managed to break into a farmer's barn and arm himself with a pitchfork, whilst me and Tim escorted a scooter riding girl that had joined us along the way from house to house, until someone reluctantly agreed to look after her.

Now on our own, we headed down a small lane through a farmyard, opening a thankfully unlocked metal gate, which gave access to a small footbridge that crossed the M5 motorway into the fields surrounding the National Trust property Killerton House. It was obvious that the fields had been recently ploughed and crossing them on a Vespa scooter in the dry was difficult enough, I can only thank god it wasn't raining because we probably wouldn't of made it. As we entered Killerton House, Tim managed to convince someone that we had been ambushed by a biker gang and needed to make a phone call.

When we eventually arrived at Exeter Police station, it was all a-buzz with police officers excitedly going about their duty, having a field day with the charge sheets they were writing up in connection with our attack. As we walked through to the interview room we saw on the floor a huge pile of boots, belts and leather jackets with denim cut offs all bearing the name Satan's Slaves.

Although the 'Slaves' had planned their ambush well, they hadn't banked on an off duty police officer being sat in one of the cars writing down all of their registration numbers.

Several months later Tim and I travelled down to the Exeter Courts to give evidence against the two remaining Slaves that hadn't been sentenced. Nervously we entered the court, and to our total amazement, saw the two defendants writing down our names and addresses as the court had stupidly posted them on the entrance door for everyone to see.

It turned out that the two we had come to help prosecute, according to them, were nothing more than bystanders, and that they were only guilty by association. Afterwards we were invited back to their local pub, where we spent the afternoon getting incredibly drunk, as both Tim and I tried to convince the two Slaves that our way of life was much more fun than theirs. Then we rode home...

Chapter 7

LOCARNO TO RAQUEL'S TO STEAMERS

Eventually the doormen at the Locarno made it very clear that mods weren't welcome any more, except on the occasional band nights. So for a short while Raquel's, just across the walkway, seemed to be the obvious alternative. Raquel's was a strange place with its biggest selling point, a cutting-edge laser show that would bring the evening to a standstill when it was periodically turned on. Disco dancers watched in amazement as the light beams danced around their heads, and rebounded off the many mirrors strategically positioned for maximum effect.

On entering Raquel's, if you asked either of the two unhelpful doormen if the club was busy, they always implied that it was. I mention this as it used to strike me as quite funny that the night-clubbers would pay their entrance fee, after being led to believe by the doormen that the club was packed out, only to go in and find it completely empty except for a few of us standing menacingly at the bar. Throughout the evening I watched people enter the main dance area, only to take one look, turn around and walk back out again. This happened quite frequently throughout the night and I often thought that, if they had all just hung around a while, the place would have filled up in no time.

Raquel's was the first place that I ever saw any sort

of truly horrific violence. One evening, myself and Colin Musty were drinking at the bar, when there was the sudden sound of the customary smashing glass, a few shouts, and a bit of a commotion. We looked around to see a guy I'd never seen before approaching us with both arms stretched out in front of him looking just like Frankenstein in some old Hammer Horror movie, with blood running down his face from a deep wound that ran all the way across his forehead.

"Where's Harvey?" he shouted, as he walked intently past us, towards the exit.

Colin and I turned back around and carried on drinking as if nothing had happened.

We heard later that the guy had smashed a glass over Andy Harvey's girlfriend's head when she told him to fuck off' after putting his hand up her skirt. So, Andy had picked up a beer glass, smashed it on the table and dragged it across the guy's forehead.

It was later that evening that I remember having my first moment of reflection when I thought, "What have we become?"

We had become so used to violence that this was just a mild interruption to a normal evening out.

Andy Harvey was always an enigma to me. It was as if he had been abducted from another planet by aliens, who very quickly decided they had made a huge mistake and dropped him off as soon as possible on the very next planet they passed. This just so happened to be planet Earth.

With its modern facilities, Bristol was like a

candle flame to coach loads of teenagers that would regularly cross the Severn Bridge to spend a drunken evening at the Hofbräuhaus, Lourdes and, of course, the Locarno and Mayfair Suite. Around 2am, Bristol city centre would be awash with welsh party goers, all in various states of undress and drunkenness. Sporadic fights and running battles would break out all across the centre, (it wasn't that unusual to see people carrying baseball bats or machetes) which the police always seemed to ignore, preferring instead to pick up the pieces rather than actually prevent anyone from getting seriously hurt.

It was on one such night that I first cast my eyes on Andrew Harvey; not that I knew who he actually was at the time, but my first sighting of him was one that has stuck in my mind for more than 35 years. Usually after we had left a club or bar, Rich would drive us all back home in his car, dropping off any girls we had managed to 'knock off' that evening. By this time I was dating a very pretty 17-year-old girl from Bath called Shelley; best friend to Steve's then current conquest, Sarah.

Shelley I always suspected would tolerate my company in the knowledge that it could assure a free lift home for her and her friends, or that we would all chip in and pay for their taxi fare. Getting everyone into the car was always a logistical problem. It would soon become very overcrowded as about seven of us would squeeze into Rich's small Skoda, manoeuvring ourselves as best we could to ensure that we had maximum female contact throughout the journey home.

On one such morning, we saw a figure that we were later to learn was Andy Harvey approach one of the Welsh coaches parked opposite the Hippodrome. For what seemed an age he stood and stared with steely intimidation at the coach's inhabitants. Then, without shifting his gaze, poetically he threw his arms down, allowing his parka to fall defiantly to the floor...

As we watched in total amazement, Andy approached the coach and climbed inside, challenging everyone one of the welsh on board 'outside for a fight'. I'm glad to say only one person got off that coach on that cold Sunday morning, and it was Andrew Neil Harvey. How could you not love that guy?

Although Raquel's provided a venue for evenings out, it wasn't really the sort of place we wanted. Many of the mods from all over Bristol had become quite well acquainted, and a new venue that was less disco and more mod, was much more desirable. Sometime in 1981 word got around that a new club had opened and that the owner was only too happy to welcome an over-excitable diverse group of teenage mod revivalists onto his premises.

Thursday evenings became Steamers nights. The club was situated just off Bristol city centre in Prince Street. Steamers was owned by a former plumber from Shirehampton called Dave Hall, and was originally planned to be a venue for various themed music nights throughout the week. When Dave announced that Thursdays would be a 60s evening for over 25s, little did he realise that his new club would become Bristol's main mod venue for mainly under 25s. With the sudden interest, for all things 1960s, the club was soon so popular, with mods that most nights, especially over the weekend, you could be sure to see any number of scooters lined up outside or on the central reservation.

Many an evening was disrupted by a police raid, not looking for drugs as you might expect, but for underage drinkers, of which there was usually quite a few. Steamers really was the place to be seen, and every night was eventful in some way or another. If it wasn't an altercation over who was going out with who or the scooters being vandalised then Avonmouth Rugby Club would turn up with the express intention of picking a fight with any mod they came into contact with. Very brave of them I always thought, as they appeared much older than us and considerably larger.

Not all the fighting was confined to the inside of the building. Sometimes it could spill out onto the streets outside. The Avonmouth rugby players on a few occasions seemed to take over the club due to their sheer numbers. Determined to make a point that it was our club and not theirs, about 10 of us patiently lay in wait outside, armed with wooden posts extricated from the roadworks opposite.

Unexpectedly out of the shadows came a skinhead full of bravado or stupidity whichever way you want to look at it, shouting at the top of his voice 'fucking mod wankers'. I'm not sure what his plan was or if he actually had one but if he did, it collapsed in a heap, before he had much of a chance to execute it. As he took off towards Princes Bridge he hadn't taken into consideration that the pavement was quite uneven, tripping over, he landing face down almost in front of us.

  Piggy once again led the vanguard as we rushed towards the now vulnerable skinhead... there was no need to join in, as it became very clear that Piggy could handle the situation all on his own. Up and down, went Piggy's fist as he pummelled the skinheads face until he was senseless, and then for good measure Piggy started to jump up on down on him.

  Very much caught up in the moment, most of us were oblivious to the sudden presence of several police riot vans that had descended on us from all directions... it was mayhem, caught unaware we all scattered as the police and their dogs came piling out of the vans. As I ran towards the centre, I noticed Dean one of the club's regulars handcuffed to one of the vans, I grabbed hold of his wrist and tried to yank it free, within seconds there was a police dog on a leash salivating at the prospect of sinking its teeth into my leg, sorry Dean but my instinct was self-preservation. Leaving Dean to his own devices I ran straight towards a woman police officer who appeared completely bewildered at all that was going on around her.

"Here hang on to this for me," I said as I handed her my wooden fence post and disappeared into the night.

The skinhead apparently survived his brutal beating with a ruptured spleen and a few other life threatening injuries. No one was prosecuted, not even Dean. We were later told that the skinhead was a known troublemaker and the police thought he deserved all that he got...

I remember being involved in many fights at Steamers some were just run of the mill and easily forgettable but some stick in my mind.

One Saturday evening I was standing at the bar with Sue Hunt and a skinhead girl, whose name escapes me. When the music was playing loudly, it was sometimes hard to talk, and so on this particular evening I made my excuses and went onto the dance floor. Halfway through the first song (which was most probably 'Shaft' by Isaac Hayes, always guaranteed to get me on the dancefloor) I noticed that Sue and her friend had got into some sort of heated argument with a black guy at the bar. Some way into the next song, I saw the black guy pull back his fist and let fly, knocking the skinhead girl to the ground. Without hesitation, I careered across the dance floor towards him. The closer I got the bigger he got. The bigger he got the more worried I got. 'This guy is huge!' I thought, but there was no stopping me now.

I was committed (and so I should have been because he was beginning to look enormous). As

I got within striking distance I found myself flying through the air, fist drawn back. He was taller than I could have possibly imagined. I had jumped as high as I could; this was the only way I was going to connect my fist with his chin.

I'd like to say at this point, that I actually gave it my best shot, a punch with such force, that in any normal circumstance would have broken the jaw of the person on the end of it, not because of any great skill in these matters but due to the momentum alone. Whoever this guy was, he was a man mountain.

As I fell to the floor I turned and looked up, only to see my target looking over me with a sort of bemusement in his eyes. As he bent over, he placed his huge hand around my neck and lifted me into the air, pinning me against the wall.

"If I ever see you, or you do anything like that again, I will kill you!" he said in a rather convincing tone.

"Yeah, yeah, yeah," I sarcastically replied.

And then he hit me…

If you have ever seen the cartoons where the dicky birds are flying around someone's head with a sort of tweeting sound, then that should give you some idea as to what it was like just before the lights went out.

I came to about five minutes later with a crowd of people standing over me; some concerned, some confused, and the majority wondering what the on earth I had been thinking.

The following Saturday, still living at Doug's mum's

house, I got out of bed and went downstairs to get some breakfast. On the way to the kitchen I noticed through the glass panel that someone was in the living room. As I opened the door I suddenly froze, as there, sitting in front of me, in my favourite chair, was the black guy from the week before. Yes the one that had threatened to kill me if he ever saw me again. To be honest I don't think he recognised me, but I felt somehow compelled to explain to him how I had managed to get the rather magnificent black eye I was sporting, and how he had played such an integral part in its creation.

It turned out, that what I thought I saw and what I actually saw, although similar, were miles apart. According to Winston, that was his name, the skinhead girl had made a racist remark towards him, and he thought she was in fact a boy, which in hindsight I can quite believe. In my defence it turned out that Winston was an ex-paratrooper who had become a bouncer, and was used to little twerps like me throwing punches at him. Winston was dating Doug's sister Fiona, and was, as far as I remember, a really nice guy. So I forgave him...

A side note to this story is the Fred Perry shirt I was wearing. I kept it as a souvenir for several years after that. Winston had left me four holes where his fingers had punctured the cloth around the collar, as he held me in mid-air against the wall.

Note to self: always pick on someone your own size or smaller.

With the Falklands war in full swing in 1982, every

one, or so it seemed was wary of anyone that looked the slightest bit foreign, just in case they were part of Argentina's fifth column, if there was such a thing. Testosterone was, for those 12 weeks of conflict, running much higher than usual, with the news media ramping up the patriotism like in any other war.

With all the patriotic fervour swirling around it seemed our brave boys in khaki could not do any wrong in the eyes of the British public, after all they had sailed the ocean blue to protect the Falkland Islanders from the invading Argentinians, whom, it would very quickly transpire, had little or no stomach for the fight ahead. But what of those wonderful boys in khaki our brave soldiers left behind? You know the ones, the ones all fired up after months of training to kill or maim anyone who got in their way.

Well sadly, Terri Bright and I were to find out one evening as we tried to make our way on foot towards Steamers nightclub. As we crossed the road we were unfortunate to witness the more unsavoury side of our khaki heroes, as a handful of them swept across the Bristol centre using their well-honed hand-to-hand combat skills on anyone who inadvertently got in their way. As we made our way to the sanctuary of Steamers, we had to negotiate our way through quite a few bodies in various states of injury, strewn across our path. Geoff, we learned, had been fighting his own private war and ended up in the casualty department of the Bristol Royal Infirmary.

The BRI was always incredibly busy over the weekend, treating all types of casualties from the evenings' drunken fall out. As Terri and I approached the desk to inquire of Geoff's whereabouts, we heard a commotion coming from the waiting area just behind us. Still etched in my memory is the sight of a very dishevelled and pitiful looking squad of soldiers looking rather sorry for themselves, covered in blood, complaining to anyone that would listen that they had been jumped as they had innocently left a night club earlier. Obviously they had tried to pick on the wrong people, whom I suspect were the Chinese bar staff from the Locarno, who we had been warned about by the manager on several occasions, because they were all well versed in everybody's favourite martial art, kung fu.

If you do the crime, do the time, don't make out that you have been unfairly attacked to save face when you have spent a good part of the evening instigating most of the trouble that eventually came around and bit you on your khaki arses.

My lovingly restored Lambretta had served me well over the years, getting me into, and, more importantly, out of trouble on quite a few occasions. But as we started to venture further afield across the UK and sometimes into Europe, it was becoming quite obvious the Lambretta was no longer up to the job. A more reliable scooter was needed.

After a while I set my heart on a second-hand Vespa that I had seen almost hidden in the back of Grays Motorcycles in Stokes Croft. Scooters as Grays were concerned were for 'little girls that enjoyed shopping trips' and if I wanted one then that's exactly what I must be. Unperturbed and quite used to such abuse I laughed it off as my main goal was to get my hands on my very own Italian dream machine. After scraping through the financial checks I managed to secure a hire purchase agreement, committing myself to the rather affordable sum of £2.50 a week over two years. After what seemed an eternity I proudly took delivery of my very own white Vespa PX125 scooter with, I'm sure to everyone's amusement at Grays, a brand new chrome back rack, that had obviously been fitted to aid me on those enjoyable girly shopping trips.

  My poor Lambretta was soon forgotten. Left to its own devices on the hard stand behind my sister's house, it slowly disappeared piece by piece. Vespa Vince would pop around quite frequently for a chat and a cigarette, usually leaving with some piece or other, a wheel here an engine there, until I was eventually only left with the once prized and sought-after crash bars, mirrors, fly screen and whip aerial. Times were changing.

  The mod revival was slowly evolving and not necessarily for the better. What had once been a free-for-all when it came to decision making as to when and where we would go, was now being controlled by an elite group that became known self impressively as the No. 1s (surprisingly there were also No. 2s although I can't remember very many people claiming to be one).

This small group of scooterists would meet up and decide on a yearly basis which seaside towns would host thousands of scooter riders from across Britain for the weekend with the full agreement of the local constabulary and council. This calendar of events was to become known as the 'official' National Scooter Runs, which still exist to this day. In effect we were becoming a rowdy version of the Caravan Club of Great Britain albeit without the luxury.

With the promise of a designated camp site and scooterist-friendly pubs most of us came to terms with this new 'grown-up approach' to what was becoming scootering rather than mod culture.

Now we were covering longer distances on a more regular basis so our style of dress started to change. Gone were the sta press trousers, loafers, boating jackets, parkas and boy next door hairstyle and in came a more road friendly, military/skinhead look of Dr Marten boots, army surplus combat trousers, MA1 Flight jackets and flat top haircuts. Although we didn't know it at the time we were witnessing the evolution and rise of a new subculture: the scooter boy.

Geoff, Mark, Andy and myself were reticent to join this new bastardisation of our neat and tidy subculture, which in reality just meant a few subtle changes in our clothing. When Cockney Simon turned up at Steamers night club one evening in a dark-green military flight suit, I knew something was afoot. If the ever-cool Simon had one then it surely must be ok?

For a while I wasn't convinced. Some army clothing was certainly more practical for long scooter journeys and also for sleeping in tents that were usually no more waterproof than our pretty useless porous parkas.

The more people that started to appear wearing this new style of clothing the more it seemed acceptable, it wasn't long before I capitulated and bought myself a nice shiny MA1 flight jacket from the ever-dependable Marcruss Stores on Hotwell Road. When I say shiny I mean shiny, it was almost a forerunner of the high-visibility jacket, although in a luminous green colour. I was gleefully informed that I looked like a highly polished olive with legs. I managed to solve this problem by fixing a long piece of string to my new coat and dragging it behind my scooter for several yards, which gave it a rather impressive, well-worn, 'been there done that' sort of look.

Chapter 8

RETURN OF THE SCOOTER BOY

I never really expected to get another scooter, but I suppose it's a bit like sex, smoking and alcohol, once you get the taste for it, it never leaves your blood, however many motorbikes, cars or racing bikes you own, for some of us scooters are a way of life.

It was almsost 30 years after the Steamers days, I'd managed to lose my job as a computer engineer after getting a surprisingly lenient one-year ban from driving.

I was the first person to get arrested in the Christmas drink driving crack down just outside Ilfracombe and according to the arresting officer I'd rolled the company car three times before it came to rest on its roof. I was under the influence of many double gin and tonics and I really didn't help matters when I jokingly gave my name as George Best and hid behind a small bush, treating the whole event as though it was some scene out of the Benny Hill Show. Apparently I was the only one who saw the funny side... that is until I woke up the next morning in an Exeter prison cell looking like something out of 'Dead Man Walking'.

I'm still not sure why I got off so lightly because on paper I could have been the poster boy for the highly publicised campaign, twice over the limit, rolling a car, giving a false name at the scene of an accident and trying to evade arrest.

I'd like to think it was because they sensed my utter shame and remorse over an incident that could have caused a huge amount of suffering and even death if it had happened in a more built up area rather than a quiet country road.

The year seemed to fly by as I went completely off the rails in what I can only describe as 'my lost year'. A year of clubs, pubs and wine bars with a small amount of food thrown in for good measure.

So by the time I was able to drive a car again, not only was I completely skint to say the least, but I'd also need a huge amount of money just to cover the high insurance premium to legally get a car on the road.

I'd seen what appeared to be an unloved scooter for sale parked outside Kellaway Motor Cycles on Coldharbour Road. Within a few days I managed to wangle a private loan and for the bargain price of £450 I was back on the road and the very proud owner of a white rusty Mk1 T5 Vespa scooter very much in need of a complete overhaul. I'd almost come full circle.

I'd had very little contact with the Scootering world since 1985 and it was interesting to see how much it had changed in the intervening years. I had abandoned my scooter and bought a trials bike once scootering had started to get more organised. There seemed more of an emphasis on attending rallies and getting pissed, than being part of anything more local. Not only had it got more organised but also started to attract the very same sub-cultures we had been fighting over the previous years – skinheads, rockabillies, and even the punks wanted a piece of what we had and were welcomed with open arms. The only rivalry was between scooter clubs. The fun, for me, had gone out of it and it was boring, unless you were into the 'drink your own piss' competitions and getting completely wasted on alcohol.

For a while I had the flight jacket, combat trousers, Dr Marten boots and full-face helmet with only the white socks serving as a reminder of where it had all begun. Scootering had become a completely different movement than the one I had originally joined.

All those years later, having a scooter again opened up a whole new social life, enabling me to reacquaint myself with friends I hadn't seen for many years and to make new ones. Scootering had changed and become much more family oriented. This, in turn, had alienated a lot of the more extreme behaviour of old, and thankfully there was not a pint of piss in sight. No more fighting on the beaches, sleeping in car parks or empty garages, this was luxury, whole holiday parks would be hired, top bands engaged and dealer spots allocated, all with an eye on the new money now flooding into scootering. I wasn't really sure if I approved or not, it seemed as if scootering had become too well organised and somewhat middle aged, I kept thinking 'what would the Michael Salter of 1979 think of scooter riding Michael Salter now?' and I knew the answer.

So what of today? Yes I still have a scooter and ride it occasionally, but sadly the exhilaration of yesteryear seems to be missing, especially where danger and excitement are concerned, we have all grown up and have children of our own.

My last brush with any real sort of trouble involving a scooter came a few years ago when a guy pulled a kitchen knife on me in broad daylight.

I was riding down Pembroke Road in Clifton when I was almost knocked off at the roundabout, when a young woman decided it wasn't my right of way. Being gracious I smiled and waved her on, only to be greeted with her mouthing 'You prick' back at me, and yes I know I could have just let it go, but I can't; I have an inbuilt idea of fairness and I was certain I wasn't a prick decided that I should inform her of the fact.

As she pulled into the Bristol University Student Union car park I tapped on her car window, and told her that actually it was her that was the prick and that I had had the right of way. What I hadn't taken into consideration was the possibility that someone else was in the car with her. An ominous voice came from the passenger side, saying 'no mate you're the prick'... 'oh shit' I thought here we go again, without a thought for my own safety 'the spirit of 79' must have kicked in, as I found myself riding my scooter into the car park and dismounted whilst removing my helmet and flight jacket. The car quickly moved forward purposely blocking off the exit, the car door opened and out stepped a six-foot tall bloke with a black eye, who certainly didn't look as though he was a stranger to trouble and by his body language was obviously intent on having a 'piece of me'.

As I approached him helmet in hand he pulled out a large kitchen knife from under the passenger seat and started waving it in controlled motions, slicing the air from side to side. Not having much experience of fighting anyone with a knife before, especially a rather sharp looking one that was in my eyes only several inches off a sword, I retreated to my scooter, started it, then drove straight at him, momentarily pinning him to the car.

I didn't actually know what I was trying to achieve but at the time it seemed the only thing I could do to try and disarm him. I got off the scooter and pulled it onto its stand, he suddenly lunged forward like Errol Flynn in The Adventures of Robin Hood, surprisingly not at me, but at the scooter, piercing the front tyre with what was obviously a very sharp knife, leaving a three-inch hole in side wall. As I stood there wondering what to do next he quickly climbed back into the car and both of them hastily departed with a screech of rubber on tarmac.

Stunned but also elated that I was still alive, I fumbled for my mobile phone and called the police. Within minutes there was a helicopter passing overhead, 'they don't hang about' I thought, after all this is affluent Clifton and this sort of thing just doesn't happen. So I waited for the sound of some sort of quick response from our ever-vigilant boys in blue, and waited, and waited, and waited.

PUNKS ON SCOOTERS

Wary that my knife-wielding adversary might soon return and I was in a quite vulnerable situation I dragged the scooter across the carpark, so that my back was against the wall, and nervously changed the front tyre with the spare.

Thirty minutes later, still no response, 40 minutes later, still no response, so out of desperation I decided to make my way to Redland Police Station which was about a mile away, just off Whiteladies Road. As I got near The Triangle I saw a patrol car leisurely coming down the hill, surely this wasn't my quick response? After all I'd just had a bloody great kitchen knife pulled on me in broad daylight in Clifton. After several attempts I managed to get the driver's attention. I tapped on the window and told the two officers of my plight and how I was the one they were obviously on their way to assist, and yes I was OK, and no I didn't need an ambulance. They both looked at me with completely blank expressions. I now realise this was due to the fact they didn't have a clue about what I was on about.

After telling them how shaky I felt, I managed to convince them that the best place to tell my side of the story was at my home, just a couple of miles away in Hotwells.

Once they were settled in my living room, I spent the next 20 minutes animatedly re-enacting the story for them. They left without taking the flat tyre or even considering the Dr Martens imprint on the front of my scooter where the knife-wielding (I suspect drug dealer) guy had tried to stop me pinning him to the car, which seemed odd as I had assumed it was all pretty good evidence. What they did leave with however was the car's registration and a promise that they would contact me as soon as they had looked into the matter.

Two weeks later I called the police station to enquire what was happening with the investigation – you know the one... man threatened by knife-wielding maniac in broad daylight... lucky to be alive.

After several minutes I managed to get a case officer on the phone to update me on what was happening with my serious (or so I thought) complaint, his earnest reply?

"Oh yes, we went around there, but they were such a nice couple I'm sure it wasn't them." I kid you not.

The case was closed.

Glevum Stax Sc

Mike Clark Scooters
53, Staple Hill Road, Fishponds, Bristol BS16 5AB.
Telephone: 656837   STD: 0272-656837

Mike Clark
Proprietor

FULL SPARES AND REPAIRS SERVICE FOR — VESPA — PUCH — GILERA — GARELLI

The Newbeats

*RUN*RUN*RUN*A'GO GO!

RUN·RUN·RUN·SCOOTER·CLUB·PRESENTS·
TAMLA MOTOWN, ATLANTIC, STAX, SOUL NIGHT
AND LIVE **MAYFAIR**
THURS 25TH JUNE   GREEN ROOMS

Douglas Poole & Michael Darby

Bristol Mods with Secret Affair, 1981
Back Row L-R: Tim Bryer, Seb Shelton (SA), Dennis Smith (SA), Neil Whitfield, Rob Merrill
Front Row: David Cairns (SA), Jon Andrews, Ian Page (SA) & Duncan Murrison

Paul Lewis from the Tredworth Green Scooter Club followed by amongst others:
Martin Weaver, Caroline Humphries and Daryl Weaver

Bristol and Dursley Mods, Torbay 1982
L-R: Annie Smith, Douglas Poole, Debbie Bendall, Kim Bailey, Paddy Smith, Catherine Tilton & Paul Harris

Gloucester modettes, circa 1982

Mod band Mayfair on stage with lead singer Jon Andrews

THE SIXTIES NIGHT RETURNS TO THE ROUNDAB[OUT]
DISCOS TO BE HELD FORTNIGHTLY FROM OCT 4th

'We've kept the Sixties going, though most of us don't remember them' D.J.

FEATURING CIRCLES AND SPIRALS LIVE ON STAGE

W.U.S.C present a 60's nite with

Mayfair

at the STONEHOUSE 22nd APRIL

A night on the town
L-R: Lin Smart, Richard Brown, Sally Smart, Unknown & Michael Salter

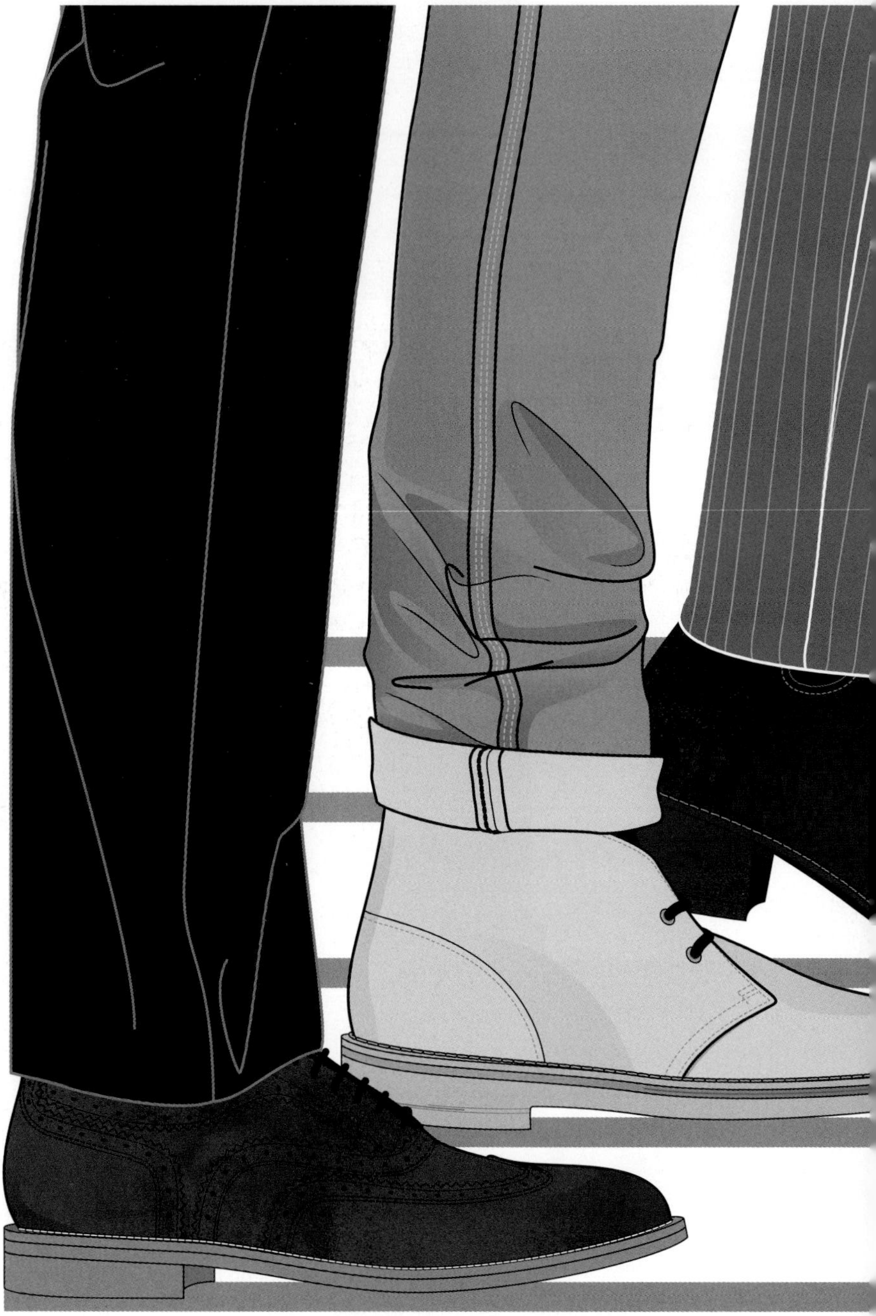

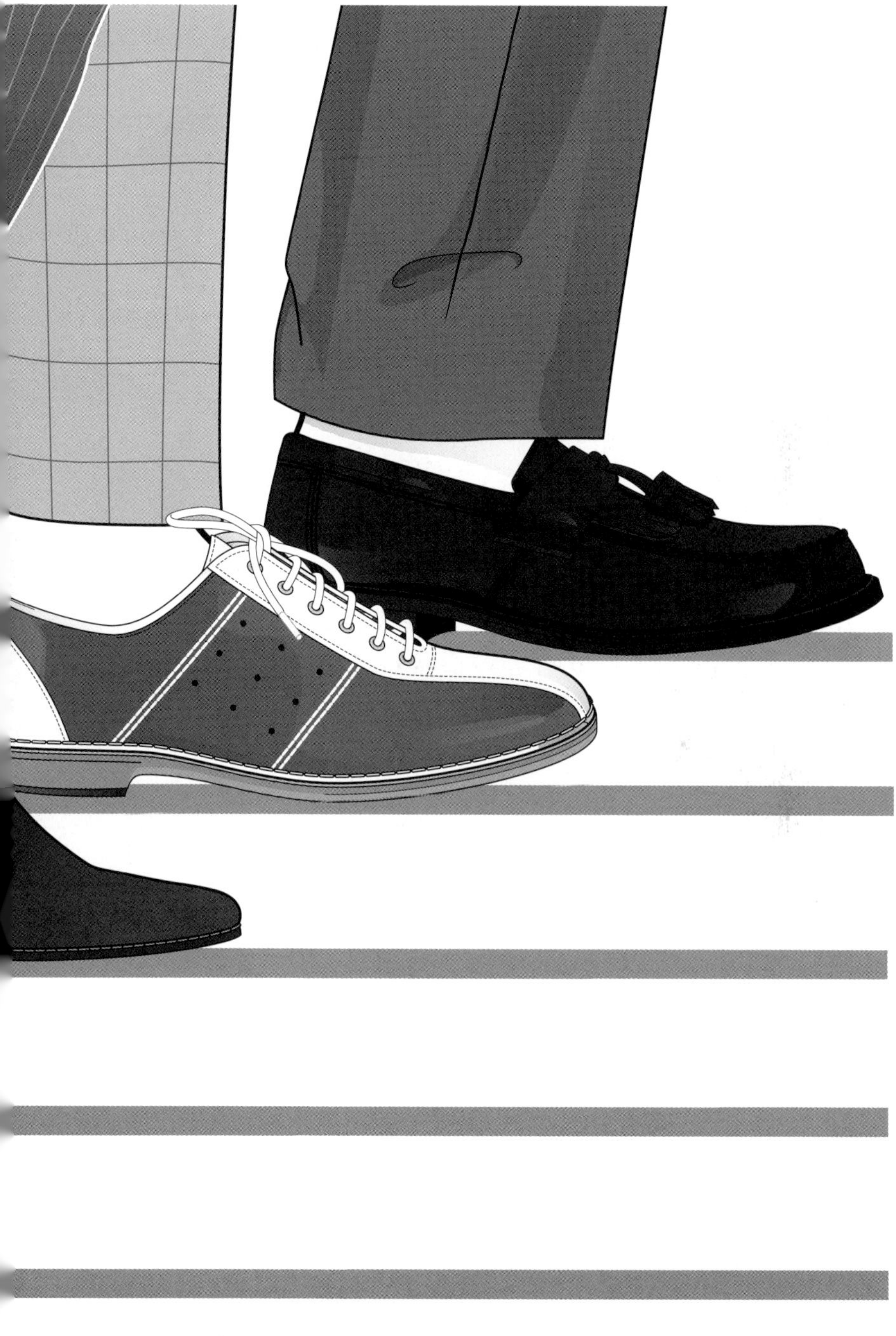

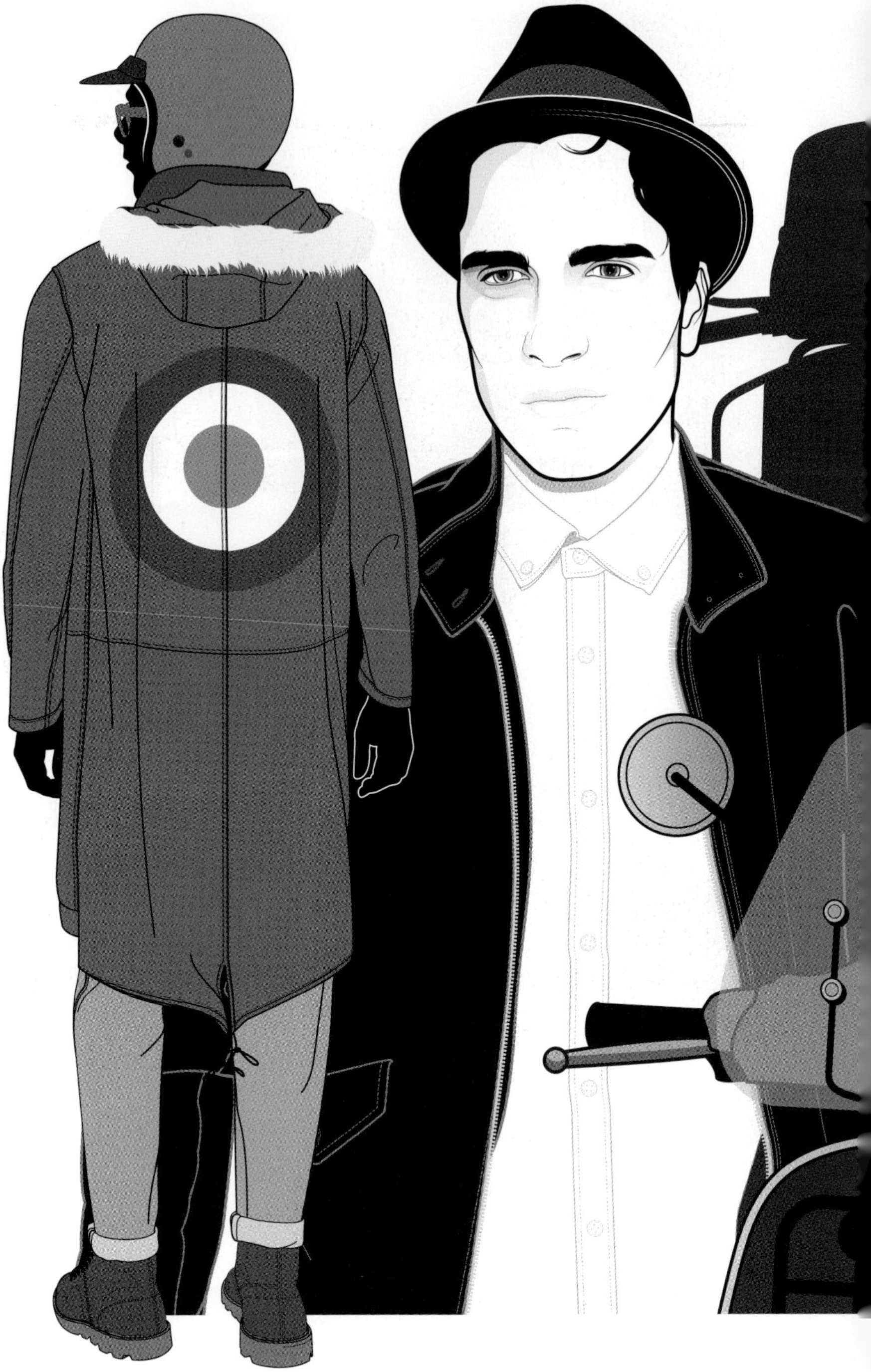

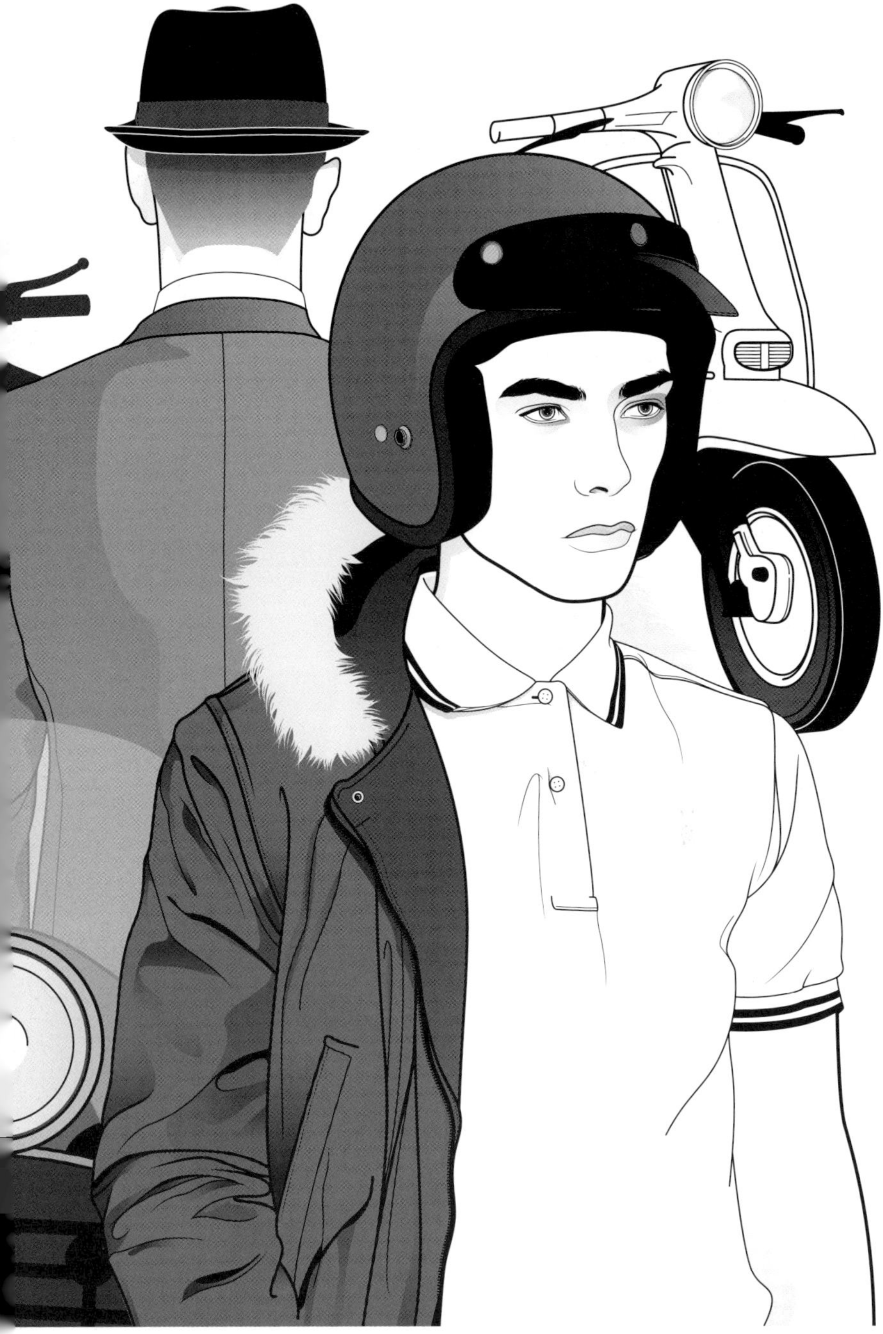

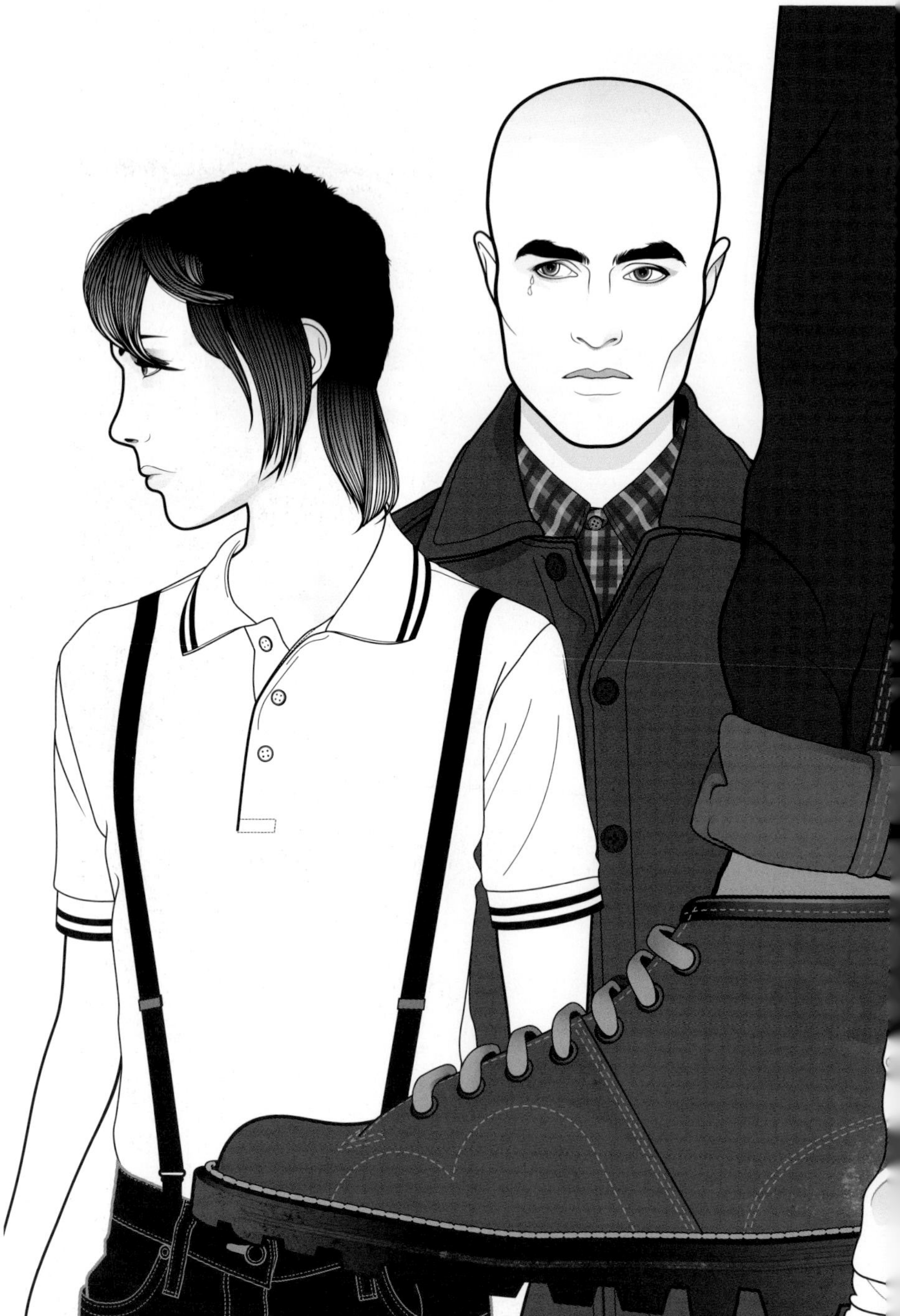

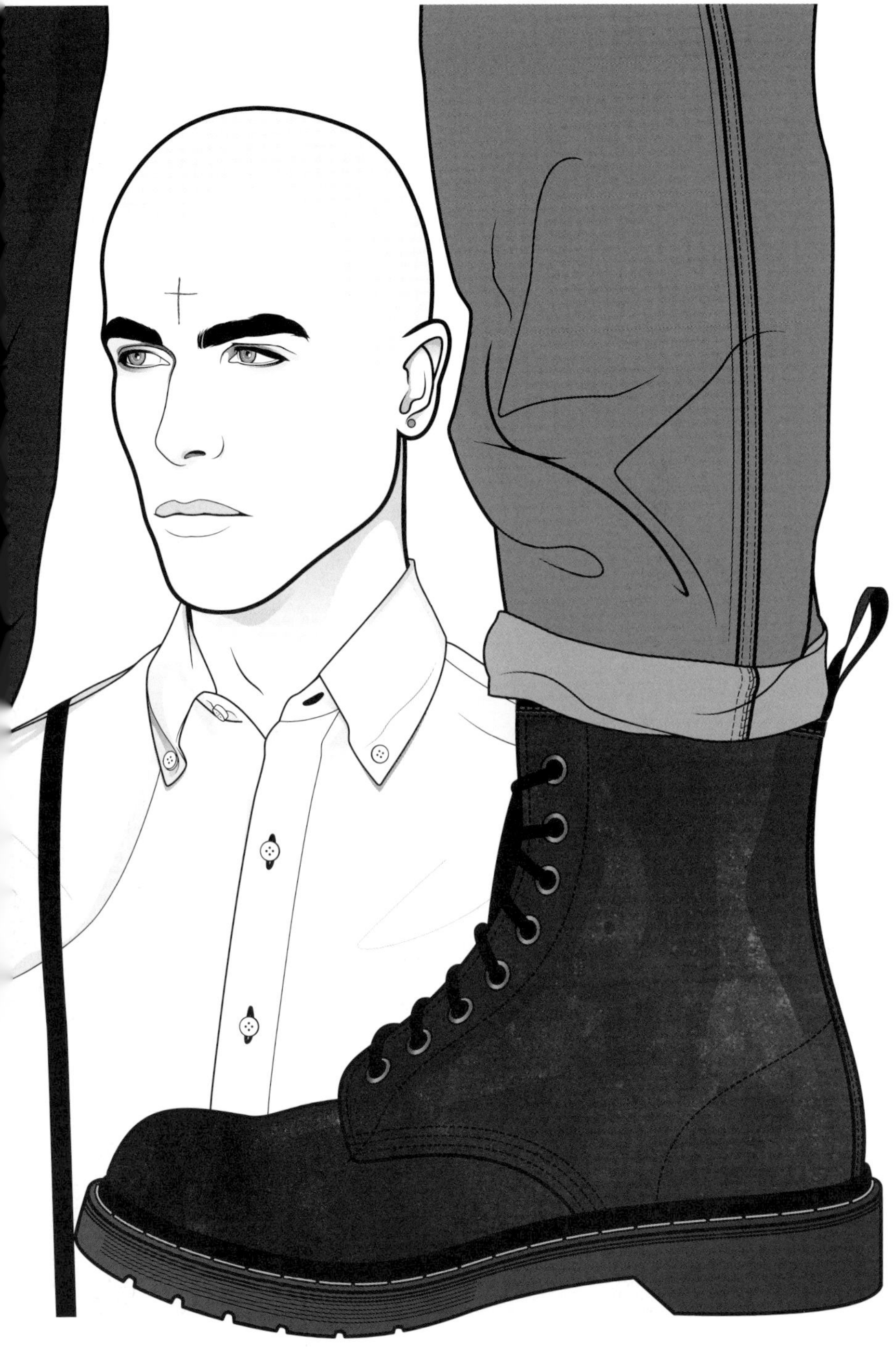

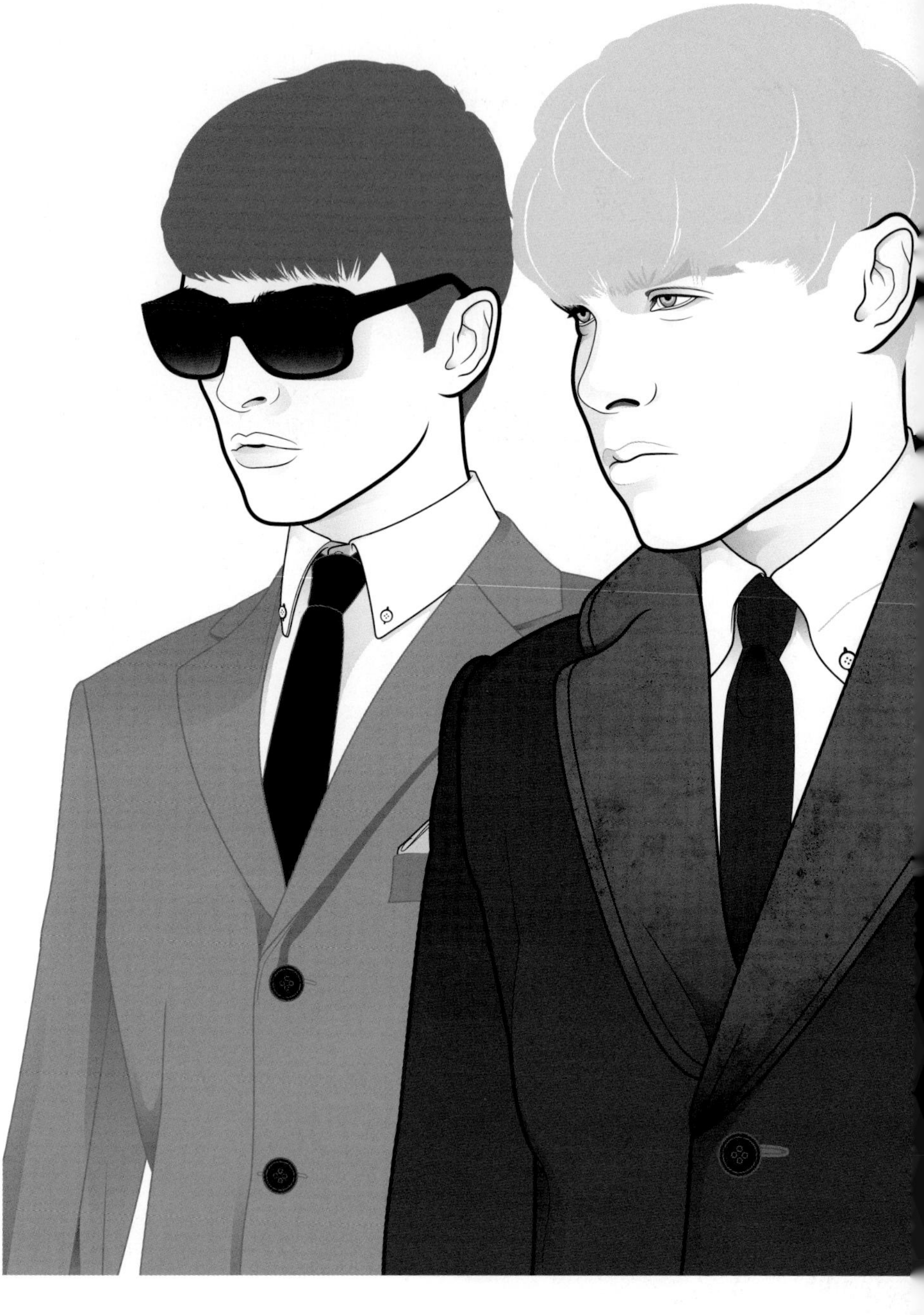

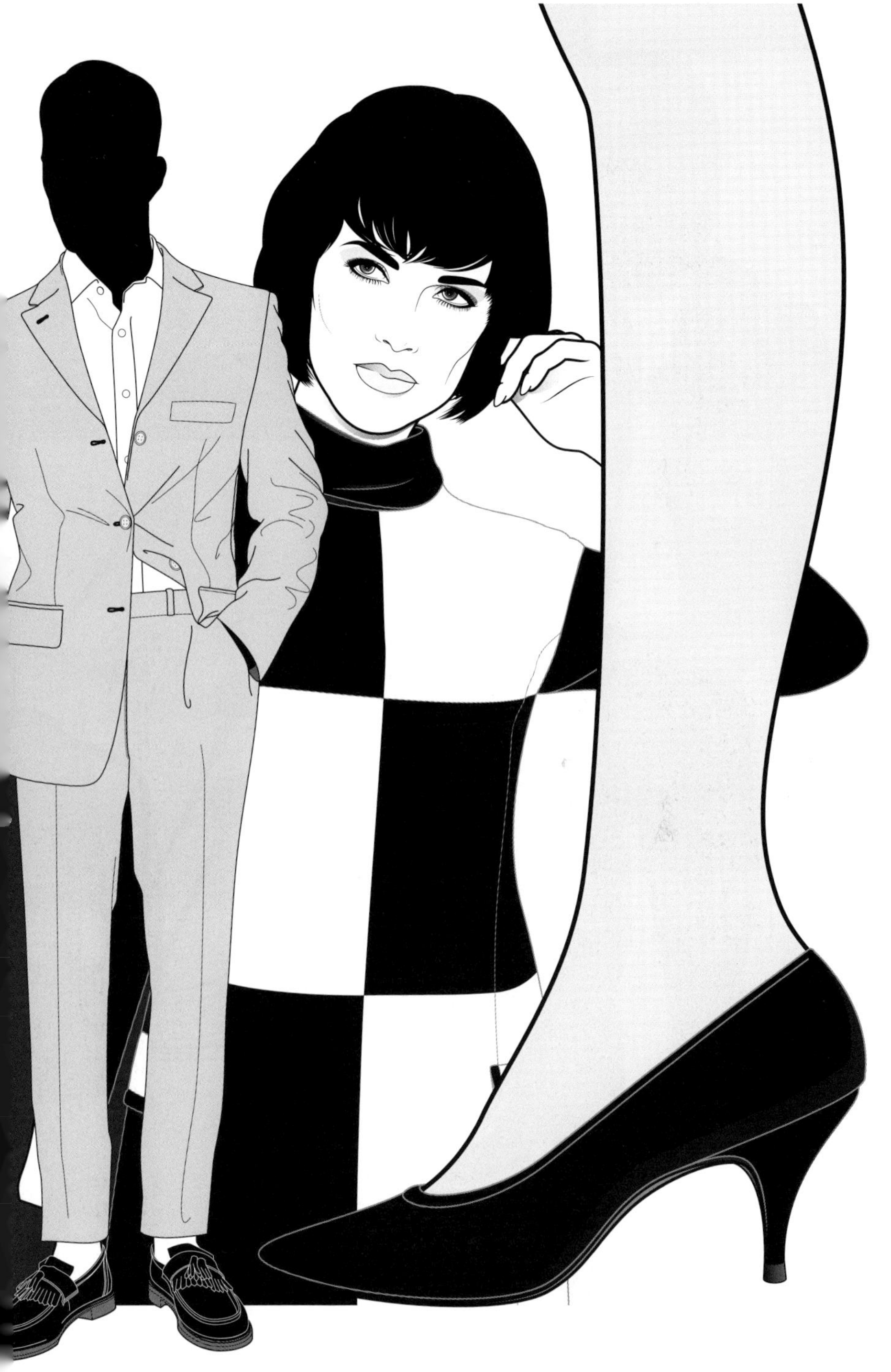

BRIGHTON
SCOOTER
RALLY
JULY 17·18 · 1982
mods
RIGHTON SCOOTER RUN
17·18·JULY — 1982 —
Mods
ISLE OF WIGHT
SCOOTER RALLY 84

NO. 1s
Jan 19
19 85
RALLY '85
BELLE VUE
The who
Scooter Run
4-6 MAY 1985
NO 2
CLACTON
50P
DO NOT IRON
Only on sale at CLACTON
DISC 85
I WAS THERE
Scooter Run
5-7 JULY 1985
No5
EXMOUTH ENGLAND
50P
Only on sale at EXMOUTH
THE WHO
QUADROPHENIA
Scooter Run
23-26 August
no.7
ISLE OF WIGHT 1985
© Paddy Smith Designs 1985
50P
Only on sale at I.O.W
DO NOT IRON

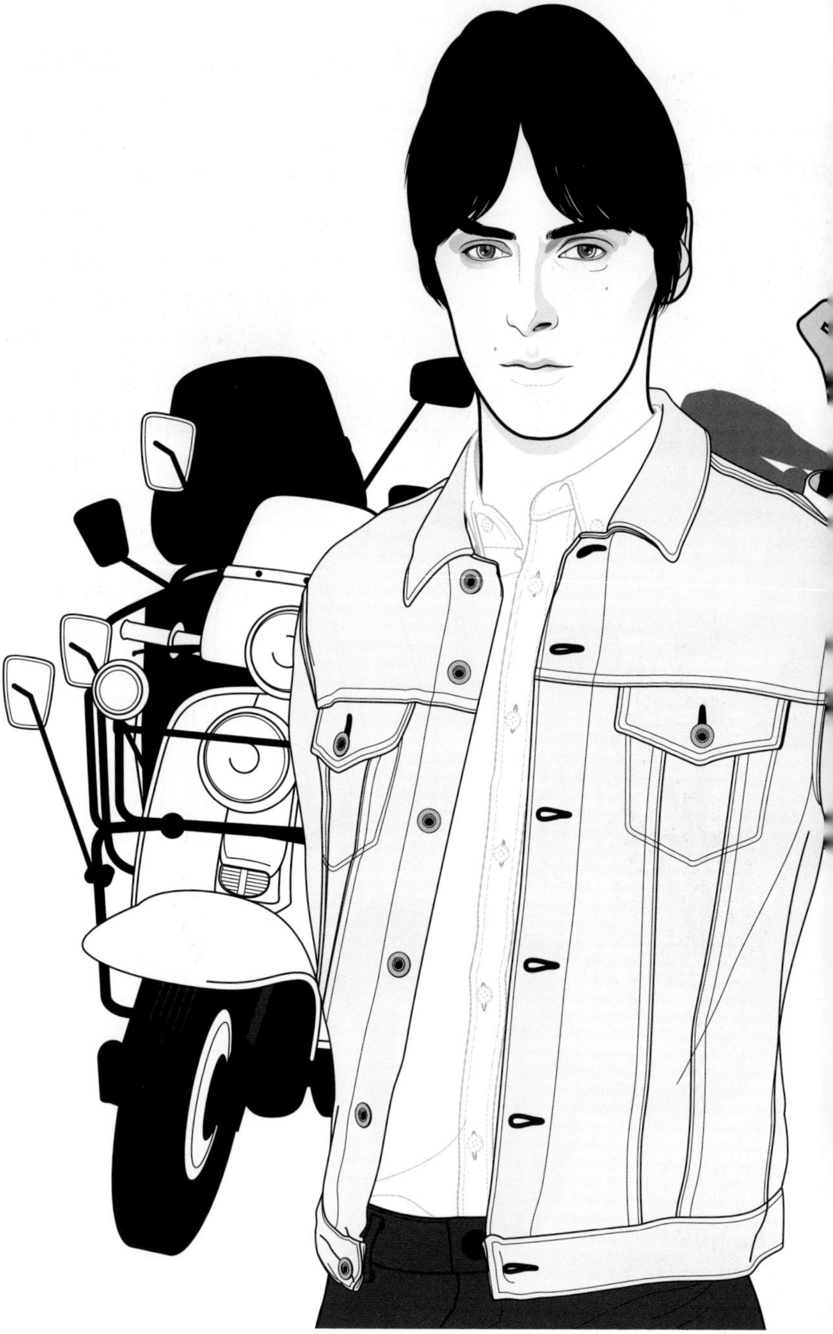

"Michael W Salter succeeds in taking us on a vivid journey through Bristol's streets and subcultures during '79-'85. As a punk, he was determined to prick the bloated balloon of prog rock, but as the scene faded in the late 70's, his 'winter of discontent was made a glorious summer' with his new discovery of the ska/mod revival. He captures the atmosphere of the violent times in acute detail, as many subcultures jockeyed for supremacy in Bristol City against a backdrop of the well-catalogued sounds of the suburbs".

PAULINE BLACK
(The Selecter)

APPENDICES

Eve Pearce, mod girl

I first became a mod at the age of 13, in 1980. My best friend at the time Alex Briggs, was dating Rob Cornish who introduced us to his friends, most of whom were mods. I went out with Mike Wollacott and started hanging out with the Lockleaze and Horfield mods better known as the BS7s Scooter Club. I lived with my mum on Muller Road, a few hundred yards away from another mod called Andy Selwood, so a lot of our time was spent crammed into Andy's bedroom listening to music and passing comment on his scooter, a nice Lambretta if I remember rightly.

There were also many nights spent at Dave Dransfield's infamous house parties, placating Marge, his mum, who was very free with clips around the ear when displeased. All the scooters were parked up on the grass outside, music pounding from inside, the neighbours must have hated us with a passion as we laughed and joked, buzzed around on the scooters and got (only a little) drunk.

One summer night that sticks in my mind was a party at somebody else's house, just down the road from Dransfield's. The party was in full swing and a few of us decided to go out for a cigarette in the large front garden. The lads were sitting on the grass, having a beer, but I decided to stay standing, in my mini skirt and parka. A couple of skinheads came swaggering down the road, spotted me and couldn't resist having a pop at the lone, young, female mod. They shouted a few lewd comments and consequently got a few back from me in a similar vein, which they took exception to.

Skinheads being skinheads are very brave in numbers, they headed towards me, obviously intent on explaining to me, the error of my ways. That was until the entire crew of mods in the garden suddenly appeared from behind the privet hedge and stood there, beers and fags in hands, staring menacingly at them. Needless to say the skinheads decided that running away was their best course of action, which they did surprisingly swiftly in their Doc Martens!

A few months later I moved to live with my dad and grandmother, and that was when I started hitting Broadmead in a big way. It didn't take long for me to start raiding my grandmother's well-stocked wardrobe for classic 60s clothes; evening dresses, boucle suits (shamefully my favourite had a real mink collar), blouses, after all it was all there for the 'borrowing'!

Mary's Café in Stokes Croft was the destination of choice for the younger mods in those days. We would take over the whole café. When we had drunk our fill of the thick frothy coffee that you could stand your plastic spoon up in, we would move up to the Hanover pub and play pool (badly) in the basement, or over to the Eclipse pub and play pool just as badly there. Next up was passing the old punk clothes shop Paradise Garage in the Bear

Pit near the bus station. This was where the punks would congregated on the benches nearby. They always enjoyed spitting at us if they thought they had the advantage of numbers.

After Paradise Garage we would wander up to St Nick's market to drool over the vintage wonders in 'Spivs'; original mod clothes, shoes, jewellery, it was all there for the buying. I quickly realised that making friends with the lady who owned the shop was a good idea and she used to put things back for me that she thought I would like, so I always got first pick. She also had a shop in Old Market that we all used to visit. As a result I quickly acquired a large quantity of vintage clothes, mainly consisting of very short skirts that my father and his friends dubbed 'Eve's pelmets'.

Having all of the right clothes was no use if there wasn't somewhere to show them off, and that's where Steamers came into the equation, with its lax over 18s policy. I think I was just under 14 when I first started going there and downing copious quantities of lager and black, or if I was feeling sophisticated, Martini and lemonade. Curiously the lads (I distinctly remember Rich Pinaccia being one of them) would all congregate at the bottom of the stairs and in a surprisingly gentlemanly way, insist on my going up the stairs in front of them. It took one of the others to finally let the cat out of the bag and reveal that their 'gentlemanly' behaviour was based purely on the fact that my skirts and dresses were so short that walking upstairs behind me provided a clear view of my knickers. Oh, the innocence of youth!

The DJ box became a frequent haunt of mine. I would stand there for ages rifling through the singles and demanding that Andy Nethercott or Andy Baker play them. In the end they just let me get on with it. I'd choose a record and cue it up ready to be played, with no care whatsoever for playlists or anyone else's thoughts on the matter. The sight of the tiny dancefloor filled with people trying to clap their hands behind their knees, whilst doing high kicks without damaging themselves or anyone else in the process was always good for a laugh.

On Steamers nights, the scooters would all be parked on the accommodatingly wide central reservation outside, always drawing attention from the passers-by. One Thursday night around 11pm, I was due to be picked up by my dad who was on his way home from hockey training. As I walked out through the group that were chatting outside, a couple of passing lads decided to kick over the first scooter, creating a domino effect, sending all the scooters crashing onto their side panels. Chaos and revenge ensued as we swiftly dealt with the offenders. It was then that I looked up and spotted my dad, the mildest of men, and his friend, advancing across the road, hockey sticks raised high, to extricate me from the melee.

Having eventually reached my 16th birthday, I persuaded my dad to lend me the money to buy a brand new Vespa 50 from Mike Clark's scooters in Fishponds. With the addition of some chrome, red vinyl lettering and heart shapes, the 'Lovebug' was born. Being one of the few girls (Maria Brown, 'Mad Marie', being the only other one who springs to mind) to have their own scooter gave me access to the usually 'lads only' pursuits, such as hanging around in Pat Evans' garage tinkering with our scooters or Pat's bubble car.

I remember we would get very drunk in Alastair Redpath-Steven's room in the Bristol University halls of residence on Stoke Lane, we would drink large amounts of cider that we had got from the Long Ashton Cider Research Centre. After we couldn't drink anymore, we would make toast on the log fire, usually resulting in burnt fingers because of our inebriated states. It was one such session that left me unable to bear even the smell of a passing pint of cider for nearly 30 years.

With my own wheels came the freedom to attend the scooter rallies and join the scooter clubs. I was an honorary Pachucio, spending many happy hours playing baseball, football or rugby on the Downs by the Sea Walls, with a gang of assorted mods. I was also somehow roped into colouring the club patches that Cath and Malcolm Beedle had got printed for the Bristol Jaguars, although I do not ever recall being a member. I only managed to attend a couple of scooter rallies; Torquay and Weston, both in 1983. The sight of so many scooters, and so many mods in the one place was amazing to us and dismaying to the local population. The police were generally pretty good natured by then, even posing for pictures with us at times, much to our amusement.

When I was 17, I moved into a flat on St Michael's Hill, over the Guitar Workshop and opposite the Gateway supermarket. Obviously a housewarming party was in order. It started on the Saturday lunchtime at noon and carried on right through the night until nearly lunchtime the next day, with people coming and going throughout, bringing more and more alcohol. That was probably one of the last times I partied with the mods. I had started work and my life was changing; it was 1984. I had been a mod for four years. Those four years were filled with friends, fun, fighting, dancing and drinking and were some of the best years of my life. We were young, we believed in something and nobody was going to stop us from having fun. I wouldn't have changed it for the world.

Geoff Rice, Bristol mod

There was more to the mod revival than just scooters, clothes and music – violence was almost an everyday occurrence. It was very rare to go anywhere without something kicking off or someone getting a bloody nose.

Being a mod in 1979 seemed to bring out the worst in nearly everyone. It was like everyone wanted to beat up a mod – very similar to the reaction the punks had stirred up a couple of years earlier. Yet in some ways the mods were the antithesis of punk: we wore much smarter clothes and certainly we looked more establishment. However, that didn't seem to make any difference, mods seemed to be the number one target for anyone who wanted to cause someone a bit of damage.

I'd be lying if I said I didn't enjoy it. The violence was something I was good at and I had no qualms about taking part in it. It was us against the world, fighting our corner against all the other gangs that were about at the same time. It was usually the skinheads that were the main threat but we gave as good as we got.

I'd say the violence wasn't like it is today: not exactly Marquess of Queensberry rules but there was a more gentlemanly way about it. No-one would pull a gun or switchblade on you, it was usually just fists, boots and beer glasses. And once the fight was over that was the end of it. There was none of this bearing grudges and reprisals, just a good honest punch up and if you lost then there would always be another day.

Like a lot of kids my age in 1977/78, I was a punk for a while when I attended St Bernard Lovell School in Oldland. I found it a good way to piss off my parents and the teachers but I always felt a little at odds with the whole thing. Whereas a lot of my friends were into The Clash and Sex Pistols, I was firmly in The Jam camp and got a lot of ribbing about how I wasn't a real punk. The Jam were a bit of an enigma, they didn't really fit in with punk.

Looking at the early album covers for inspiration which we did a lot in those days I found I had more of an affinity with The Jam ones, like *Modern World* and *All Mod Cons*. I thought the smart suits and retro 60s clothing Weller, Buckler and Foxton were wearing, was more me than the punk styles of safety pins and bondage trousers, especially the ones that were then being churned out in such places as Paradise Garage in the Bear Pit.

I didn't really see how I was going to get a girlfriend with a safety pin stuck through my nose, so I started making little changes in smartening up my dress sense, which pleased my parents and school teachers no end.

I suppose a lot of things started to change for me when a few of my school mates offered me a tarted-up 1964 Series 3 LI 150 Lambretta scooter for £150 which they had 'acquired' somehow. In those days that was a huge amount of money, probably about £1000 now. Luckily my mum had been saving with the 'Pru' and with a bit of badgering she got me the scooter. I was only 15 and rode it back from Longwell Green to Cadbury Heath without a crash helmet. I was so naïve! I didn't realise you had to wear one or even know how to handle the thing.

I was completely illegal but that didn't stop me riding it. I'd push it out of my house, around the corner then when I was out of sight from my parents I'd start it up and ride it to school where I would feel like the bee's knees as I pulled up at the gates. I'm not sure if my mates were jealous, or thought I'd sold out, and to be honest I didn't really care. I was now a fully-fledged mod, especially now I had my very own scooter.

My parents were completely unaware I was riding the scooter, as I had convinced them I was taking it to school for an art project. That is until I got nicked by a special constable. This sort of set the scene for me over the next few years as I was always getting in some sort of trouble, especially with the police.

I soon hooked up with a guy called Andy Smith who lived nearby. He had a Vespa P200e and we started hanging around the streets of Banjo Island near where I lived. It was a pretty rough place in those days, especially if you had a scooter and were wearing the sort of clothes I was – Levi jeans, desert boots, Fred Perry shirt and a parka, which was like a 'red rag to a bull'. Anyone and everyone seemed to want to either kick you off or hit you with something.

In the late Seventies it was hard to get hold of anything resembling mod clothing. Just like the punks we were dictating the fashion, so it was a while before the big clothes manufacturers caught up. A few of the more clued-up mods like Malc were getting their suits made to measure but that was big money if you wanted a really good one as it was nearly a month's wages.

  I couldn't really afford that sort of money because I was only a butcher's apprentice working for Dewhurst so had to make do with what I could scrape together. I did eventually get some decent mod-style clothes but the suits were borrowed from a mate whose step dad was a tailor and had a shop on Lower Ashley Road. As they were only on loan, I was careful to keep them from getting ripped or damaged. My own clothes were always getting ruined from the fighting or coming off my scooter, which seemed to happen quite frequently.

  What was funny about wearing a suit was that your parents had one less thing to nag you about. Whereas before they were always banging on about my scruffy punk dress and being part of the punk movement, they couldn't really complain about what we were wearing as mods because we were in a lot of cases taking pride in our appearance, more than they were. Wearing a suit in the early 80s was a statement, even more so than the 1960s mods, because in those days most people wore them. It was just that the original mods tried to be that little bit more sharp, and later on flamboyant.

  Eventually me and Andy stumbled across The Jolly Cobbler pub on Chiphouse Road in Kingswood. It was like a drop-in centre for scooterists. You never knew who was going to turn up, friend or foe, and it wasn't always the skinheads that came looking for trouble. Sometimes the pub's locals would have a go at us. You always had to be on your guard in those days. Trouble was always on the agenda even in places you would have thought of as relatively safe.

The Cobbler was the sort of place that you could meet like-minded people and chat about clothes, music, scooters, and where was the best place to get parts for your scooter. Mirrors were sepecially hard to find in the early days, although me and Andy found a cheap solution by 'borrowing' them off people's cars. There were still some of the old type ones about, like the 1960s Hillman Imp. Once we unscrewed them we would try and attach them to our scooters, which wasn't always that successful.

That was only a short-term problem because we soon discovered Mike Clark's Scooters in Fishponds. Mike Clark's had a lot of original stock from the 60s, everything that everyone wanted, and he wasn't shy about charging a small fortune for it. But we all still went there as it was the only place we could get the sort of stuff we were after. Mike Clark must have thought he'd hit the jackpot when the mod revival happened because every Saturday there were always a load of mods outside, eager to spend some of their weekly wages in his well-stocked shop.

It became a bit of a meeting place for a while but

most of the time, even in winter, we would hang around outside the Jolly Cobbler, very rarely going inside. A lot of us were blatantly underage where drinking was concerned but that didn't stop us getting hold of alcohol, especially when we started visiting the clubs in Bristol.

Lourdes nightclub in Fairfax Street was the first mod night me and Andy attended. As far as I know, it was the first club to hold a 60s night catering predominantly for the mod crowd. I was only 16 but managed to get in wearing jeans, a Ben Sherman shirt and Harrington jacket. I'm quite short especially up to the bouncers who seemed massive and I don't think they noticed what I was wearing. The music wasn't exactly mod as it was more 60s chart music, but in those days you would travel anywhere if you thought they would be playing Motown, The Who or even The Jam, which I remember they played a lot of at Lourdes, especially 'The Dreams of Children'. Strangely Adam Ant was pretty cool in those days and the mods really took to 'Kings of the Wild Frontier' which was always guaranteed to pack out the dancefloor. The lyrics sort of summed it all up really: 'We are the family'.

But the 'daddy of them all' was Steamers night club. Ask any mod from that time and you would be hard-pushed to hear a bad word said about it. Bad things happened, yes, but when you're a teenager and growing up fast, all these things are part of your initiation into becoming an adult, or at least they were in those days. The world seemed a hard, violent place and you felt you had to stand up for what you thought was right otherwise you would get trampled on. Life in those days seemed as though it didn't take prisoners.

There could be 50 or 60 scooters sometimes outside on the road or central reservation. Thinking about it now, the club was just far enough away from the centre, so that it wasn't discovered by the hundreds of Welsh that would descend on the New Bristol Centre over the weekend, which inevitably ended in punch ups. If they had realised we were just around the corner I suspect it would have been a massacre: no one would have been left standing.

Steamers was like a social club as well as a night club. The owners really liked us and backed us to the hilt if there was any trouble. Of course they were making a lot of money as the place was jam packed but I like to think it was more than that, that he actually liked having us there. It certainly was never dull.

The Avonmouth Rugby Club players turned up quite a lot, looking for trouble which inevitably ended up in some fight or other. I had my fair share and bounced a few people off the walls. An evening in Steamers wasn't complete unless there was a punch up about something. There must be hundreds of stories that involved someone getting hurt or a place smashed up during that period. Although we didn't always go looking for trouble we did have our fair share when it came to starting it.

Sometimes just a dance could spark off a fight

and someone getting a good hiding. Mangotsfield Rugby Club was the venue for a birthday party, and a few of us went with some of the girls who hung around the Cobbler pub. You could tell as soon as we got there we weren't welcome, as the looks we got from a group of locals weren't exactly friendly. There was definitely a nasty atmosphere which went on all through the night. We were all sat to the right of the dance floor with a bunch of locals on the left. The more we seemed to be enjoying ourselves the more pissed off they seemed to get.

To be honest I think it would have all just come to nothing if the DJ hadn't put on the Stray Cats single 'Rock This Town'. We had been up dancing to some Tamla Motown and a bit of mod music, not taking it at all seriously as we were out for a laugh. But when the Stray Cats came on, the locals sort of turned it into some sort of dance-off. They were jiving and bopping around like some demented acrobats, I assume to make some point or other. What none of us expected was Vespa Vince to get up and join them. I don't think I remember seeing Vince dance before that but I can tell you it was a sight to behold. Where he learned to dance like that I'll probably never know, but it was brilliant. He just dominated the dance floor like some professional rockabilly dancer, if there is such a thing. We of course not only thought it was brilliant but also highly entertaining, especially at the locals' expense. They were not happy at all and that was the catalyst. No blatant provocation or anything, just some bloke dancing, but in those days that could be more than an excuse for a punch up.

After a bit of shoving and pushing on the dance floor I went up to join Vince, just to show a bit of moral support. After a bit of verbal with some well-known hard-nut it all quietened down, the lights came on and the music stopped. Obviously it was time to go. We thought that was the end of it. What we didn't realise was that we were being followed by the hard-nut and two of his even bigger mates.

Eventually I just had to turn and accept I wasn't getting home without getting a beating, so I did what I thought was the best thing to do and I confronted the one that was mouthing-off most. He threw the first punch which caught me around the side of the head. To my surprise it wasn't as bad as I thought it was going to be and I managed to ride it.

We ended up rolling around on the floor, throwing punches at each other until I got the better of him. His two big mates just stood there not knowing what to do. Eventually I managed to get my knees on his arms and pin the mouthy one down. Grabbing his hair and ear I just 'snapped' and repeatedly smashed the back of his skull into the ground as hard as I could. Luckily for him the police turned up. If they hadn't I don't think I would have stopped until I had just an ear and a piece of hair in my hand. I was so wound up.

Lucky for me, the copper was the father of a friend of mine. He lifted me up by my hair turned me around and said, "Right Geoff, I think it's time for you to go home now." I was later told the bloke was charged with inciting violence or something, quite ironic really as he was the one on the receiving end, but he would have done the same to me if he had had the chance.

Another story I recall was when about ten of us were riding down from The Jolly Cobbler pub into Bristol one evening. Andy Baker, Andy Smith, Rich Pinaccia, Piggy, Phil, Vespa Vince, Tim, Darron and a few I can't remember now, all on our way to Steamers. As usual we were messing about enjoying riding our scooters, going around the keep left bollards, just being silly buggers, causing a nuisance. We were really oblivious to anyone else using the road, blocking most of it. Just as we were going through Whitehall, a car, I think it was a Ford Escort, aggressively came up behind us. Understandably, the car driver was getting really fed up and cut us up in an effort to get past but he hadn't taken the traffic lights into account.

Looking back he didn't do anything that we wouldn't have done in the same situation but for him it was wrong decision; wrong time, wrong place.

"Right you bastard," I thought, as we descended on him. Before he had a chance to move off, we all surrounded his car and went about destroying it. Andy Baker went in first with his Cuban-heeled Beatle boots smashing in all the lights. I took out the screwdriver I carried in my parka pocket and went about trying to puncture his tyres. When that didn't work I climbed up on the car and tried to kick in his windscreen. As I only had desert boots on that didn't go too well either so I resorted to jumping up and down on his bonnet. It was mayhem. Luckily for him we couldn't get into his car, as I hate to think what would have happened to him if we had. He must have been terrified. Because he was our age, we felt it was right to wreak some revenge on him, and admittedly it was disproportionate to what he had done, but that's what it was like then. As we rode off I looked back at the carnage we had caused. I must admit I had a smile on my face as it reminded me of that gang film *The Wanderers* where the bloke says, "Don't fuck with the Wongs," but in this case it was "Don't fuck with the mods". We were proud of being mods and being someone: no one was going to push us around.

With the rise of the scooter boy and interest in northern soul music, many of us started distancing ourselves from the mod revival. I just sort of went along reluctantly with the crowd but never really lost my mod leanings. The Mayfair Suite in the New Bristol Centre and The Rockpile club near Temple Meads became the new places to socialise. We sort of just moved on, forgetting Steamers. There was still the odd break out of violence but it was getting less and less as the different sub cultures integrated: the skinheads, rockabillies and even punks were getting scooters and starting to turn up on the 'runs'.

With the skinheads infiltrating 'the scene' it all started to get too political for my liking; very right wing with a lot of National Front overtones. The fun had gone out of it. The skinheads ruined what had been a great way to spend your youth, and made it into something quite ugly. And so I rode out to a place called Beach in Upton Cheyney, and ceremoniously pushed my scooter into the river by the bridge, holding it down until it was totally submerged.

This was my way of saying goodbye to those days, not unlike Jimmy in *Quadrophenia* when he launched his scooter off Beachy Head.

I walked home thoroughly depressed.

Jon Andrews aka **Jonny Locomotion**,
lead singer of Mayfair

It was the Summer of 1978, I was 18 years old. I was not into any particular fashion, but always followed soul music in the pubs and clubs in town. I had ridden mopeds and motorcycles for a few years, and had recently sold my bike to finance the deposit for an apartment I wanted to rent, I was also on the lookout for some cheap transport, and a work colleague suggested that I could purchase his old Lambretta scooter that had been garaged for six years for 30 quid.

It was a 1970 GP150 Italian Innocenti Lambretta, it looked in fairly good nick, and was bedecked with two whippy tank aerials, front crash bars, trumpet out-rigger exhaust and a white fly screen with black sticky letters "BRISTOL" on the front, I immediately identified it as a suedehead scooter, it fitted the time line, and I had seen one similar when my elder sister had a relationship with a suedehead in 1972. He used to take me for rides on the back of his scooter which I enjoyed immensely.

Now here is where the love started, we pushed the scooter out into the garden, pumped air in the tyres gave it a small drink of petrol, and within three kicks it had started! I found that so incredible – it had not been started for six years, none of my past bikes would have done this.

So off I set, I got used to the hand controls quickly, and the burble and splutter of the out-rigger exhaust was a joy. I was having so much fun.

A few months later whilst riding around Bristol's Old Market, I saw two guys on scooters in front of me, I pulled alongside them at the traffic lights and spoke to them, we pulled over for a chat and I recognized one of them as Cockney Tony, I had seen him a few times in the pubs and clubs in town, the other guy just sat on his scooter and said nothing, Tony introduced him as Zulu, both were wearing original US fishtail parkas and he started to tell me about how mod was about to make a comeback. I was hooked from that moment and embraced it fully.

Actually, It was not hard for me to embrace mod because it was already in my genes. As a very young lad I can remember going to see *A Hard Day's Night* at the cinema in Bristol, and I loved Merseybeat music – even aged five I could recite whole songs from many of the 60s artists of the day. So when mod fully re-flowered in late 1979, I already knew many of the musical anthems off by heart and had a good grasp of what being a mod was all about.

Mod was slowly gathering pace and publicity in early 1979 and then exploded onto the scene mainstream mid-way through 1979 with the likes of The Specials and Madness, this brought the masses to the mod revival, but personally, I did not have a real liking for ska music, and considered it to be more a skinhead vibe than mod. Suddenly there was an abundance of people who thought they were mod just by wearing cheap non-mod German

APPENDICES

parkas bedecked with Ska Man and other two-tone imagery. I considered this to be the work of the devil, sent to spoil true mod etiquette, culture and class.

In 1979 if you wanted something, you had to get off your ass to get it! There was no online ordering, no mobile phones, just you and the big outdoors, I spent hours scouring War On Want and other charity shops looking for mod clothing from the 1960s and there was still an amount of good stuff available. I used the book *Mods* as a style reference because this was considered the book of sacred knowledge by many.

I had acquired an original US parka, and by now had quite a good selection of original mod clothing, which was mostly secondhand, I was still going to a few of the pubs and clubs in town and was frequenting the Dug Out club on Park Row. It was an anything goes type of place, full of all walks of life and fashions – punks, rastas, you name it, you could find it.

On one visit to the Dug Out with mod being very much in the minority of visitors I saw a fellow mod propping up the bar in the far corner with his girlfriend, I went to speak to them and immediately struck up a good friendship with them both, we started to meet each week at the Dug Out for a few months or so, his name was Steve Dixon, and his girlfriend was Alison. I was a north Bristol lad and Steve was from Whitchurch, he was the first of many friends I made from the south of the River Avon.

It was Steve who suggested that I should visit the Horse and Jockey pub in Frogmore Street, where the mods were starting to gather in small numbers, and I agreed to meet him there the following Friday night.

The pub is old, very poorly presented and alongside Bristol Ice Rink an area of Bristol that was, at that time, very well populated till the late evening. On arriving, I found only one scooter parked up. I was quite nervous, I parked a little way up the hill walked down and pushed the door to the bar open. The first person I saw was Andy Harvey, this was a good sign, because me and Andy were friends from a few years back. Slowly more mods arrived, and I got to meet Dennis Lane, Cockney Simon, Seamus, Brad Veale, Foxy, Fred, Neil, Andy Nethercott, the numbers grew and the beer was flowing.

Then, about 9.45pm a shout rang out that the Welsh were outside, the pub emptied and there was a mass brawl outside with Andy Harvey and Steve Dixon leading the Bristol mod front line. When it was over everybody returned to the pub to celebrate the triumph over the Welsh. I found out later that this was a regular thing as the Welsh would come over by the coach load for ice skating and when this had finished at 10pm they would march outside looking for trouble. This was all so new to me, but I had to get used to it quickly because the late 70s were violent times and being a mod, trouble and violence followed you on a near daily basis. I can recall that Steve Dixon had a particular penchant for the Welsh, and never passed up the opportunity to exchange blows with them.

The mods from the Horse and Jockey, were the only group that truly united and represented Bristol mods as a whole, and went on to form the backbone of the Westside Unicorns Scooter Club that at its peak in 1980/81 boasted more than 200 members from all over Bristol and surrounding areas. Bristol began to develop a good number of scooter clubs, but most of them were small, local groups with between 20 and 50 members.

As the Westside Unicorns, we embarked on many National Scooter Rallies in the early days and forged strong relationships with fellow scooter clubs such as Glevum Stax, Cheltenham Blue Diamonds, Dursley Scooter Club and Weston & Clevedon. The Unicorns were in fact, one of the biggest supported scooter clubs in the UK at that time.

At this point, any of my more local friends that had not subscribed to the mod anthem were ruthlessly cast aside, as I went in search of new friends with a like-minded adoration of mod, it did not take long, on a visit to Tiffany's night club for a party, I met some fellow mods who were from the nearby Redland area of Bristol. These mods were (like me) really into the fashion, music and scooter side of mod. They were largely from the Henleaze, Horfield, Cotham, Redland and Bishopston areas of north Bristol, but as a group, they mainly kept to themselves.

So, I had two different groups of mod friends, It was a balancing act on my part, I had my friends from the Coach pub and Westside Unicorns, which were a diverse group from all over Bristol and my more local mod group. It was rare that the two groups met or participated in the same mod events being locally held, having said that, people did tend to stick to their own area's back then, and it was the Westside Unicorn group that truly put Bristol mod on the move.

In late 1979, at a party held by my local mod friends, it was decided to form a band. It was early days, there was a drummer, a guitarist and a bassist, but no singer. I stepped up and began to sing 'Heatwave' and 'Midnight Hour', word for word. I got the job and the band started to rehearse on a regular basis and was named Mayfair.

One of the more memorable gigs that we participated in was a battle of the bands held at Trinity Hall in Old Market. It was quite well publicised and had several high-profile judges. I recall that I performed with my arm in plaster due to a fall down the Bristol Royal Infirmary Hospital staircase after a night drinking in the Dug Out club. I had only gone to the hospital to get a coffee before the three-mile march home. Yes it can happen!

Back to the gig... each band performed two songs, there were five bands and we were the last act. Several members of the band, like me, enjoyed a drink or three, and by the time it came for us to take the stage most of us were near inebriated. We started off well, and after our fourth song people were running around trying to get us offstage.

But we were having fun and carried on for another song or two. Finally when the judging took place we were placed second but were eliminated from the competition. We had a manager at the time, who I can only remember as Mark, he said that one of the judges was from Status Quo and was impressed with what he saw and heard and invited us to go to London to visit his studio. I remember thinking 'Status Quo! are you joking! Rockers!' We declined the invite citing musical differences, how things may have changed had we gone.

Mayfair performed regularly on the local club circuit, the Stonehouse, Green Rooms, Hope Chapel, Trinity Hall, Steamers and the Bierkeller, and as the band gathered momentum in 1981 we played further afield in Swindon, Gloucester, Cheltenham, Worcester, mainly in tandem with a mod event or mod disco. Mayfair also supported Amen Corner (1960s band), Small World (mod revival) and The Alarm.

Although The Alarm were a pop/rock band, we did the gig because they were Number One in the charts with the single 'Sixty Eight Guns'. We had a great reception at The Alarm gig, and we got the crowd going so well that The Alarm roadies decided to turn the sound down so The Alarm would sound louder. It was a bit petty on their part, but talking with The Alarm back stage, they came across ok, and boy did they have some guitars! I counted 12.

Only about 10 people came to watch Amen Corner at The Bierkeller, which was a massive disappointment for them, in fact it was just their mates. I remember thinking, does nobody remember 'If Paradise Is Half As Nice'? Around 200 people came to see Mayfair, yet we were the support act. About half way through our set the place emptied as the audience took part in a mass brawl outside.

  Mayfair were interviewed live on BBC Radio Bristol because the presenter of the show had some wild idea that the rise of Mayfair was as a result of The Jam splitting up. What a laugh! Conway, our drummer, pissed off our mod followers by claiming that only a few mods came to see us play, it was not true. He said it in the hope that Mayfair could attract a wider audience, it was his idea and not mine. I spent a good few weeks getting blamed for those words, and it hurt at the time because our mod following was absolutely superb – we used to get coaches of fans from Weston, Clevedon and Gloucester come and see us.

  The presenter asked us what our main influence was and I replied Carling Black Label, which brought a good few laughs around the studio. At the end of our interview they played our track 'Traffic', and as we marched out of the studio, another Bristol band was waiting their turn to be interviewed, one of them turned round to me and said, 'and we are supposed to follow that', quite a compliment I thought. I wished them all the best as we glided out of the studio to the nearest pub.

  One of the main reasons that Mayfair managed to

produce some decent material was that all of our musical equipment was top notch. I played a Fender Precision bass guitar with a jazz neck, it was really a top guitar with a great sound, it belonged to the guitarist who played a Fender Telecaster. He also had a Hoffner Violin Bass just like Paul McCartney, similarly the drums were high quality as were our amps and PA system, it really helps to make a good sound. We also had a great place to practise, that also was a big plus. It was my father's old boat building warehouse, we named it 'The Boathouse' and practised there twice a week. Many people used to come along to the practice mainly for a laugh, or to catch up with what's happening, and of course for the beer afterwards.

My musical influences were absolutely The Small Faces and The Kinks and I also liked The Searchers, The Who, The Beatles, Stones, Animals, Spencer Davies, Manfred Mann, Troggs and Zombies.

Of the mod revival bands, the only stand-out band for me was Secret Affair, followed by The Jam, Back To Zero and The Purple Hearts, that's it!

I swapped my beloved GP150 Lambretta for musical equipment, an Orange amplifier and speaker cab that I used for band practice. I also managed to buy a Lambretta GP200 from a chap called Rocky. This scooter forms the basis for the 'Locomotion' scooter that I still have today.

In fact, from 1978 to 1984 I manage to own a good few scoots: a Lambretta GP150, GP200, SX200, LI150 and Vega 75, and from Vespa an SS90, PX125 and P200E.

Not content with the scooters as my only form of mod transport, I upped my quest and managed to procure a 1963 BMW Isetta Bubble Car, I had it re-sprayed in blood red, added a tank aerial with must-have fox tail, and had a windscreen sun visor strip made with The Kinks emblazoned on it. I also changed the seat cover for a Union Jack, it was awesome!.

Being such an elderly vehicle, it had many quirky defects, I can recall the gear shift on the steering column often fell off, leaving me stuck in gear, or stationary until I was able to screw it back on. It had a vinyl sunroof that never kept the rain out and the lights only worked in good weather. Quite often I would get pulled over by the police, just for a chat about the car.

The Isetta battery was a regular car size one located directly underneath the bench seating. One day I was driving down the Gloucester Road on a busy Saturday when the Bubble suddenly began to fill with smoke. I quickly pulled over to the side of the road, opposite Duck Son & Pinker piano shop on Stokes Croft and me and my friend bailed out much to the amusement of passers by.

I could see that smoke was coming from under the seat, and then I saw flames. I quickly opened the door and ripped out the bench seat and threw it a few yards from the Isetta ablaze. I called my friend (Just The Job Rob) for help, but he was too busy rolling around on the floor in hysterics. The cause of the blaze that destroyed the seat (and my pride) was that a plastic protective cover that fitted on top of the battery had fallen off. Every time we went over a bump, the battery terminals shorted out on the metal springs on the underside of the seat which then led to sparks, that finally set fire to the horse hair padding in the bench seat. Incredible but all true.

On another and more serious occasion, I had driven my Bubble to meet the local mods at Small Park in Henleaze, there were about 10 of us sat around the park, having a few beers and chatting, when a large group of skinheads arrived and a serious row broke out. One of the mods had some bad blood with one of the skinheads and smashed a beer bottle over the skin's head. I remember him crumpling to the floor. A full-scale fight broke out which left several in our party needing hospital treatment, it was the same for the skins. A shout went up that the police were on their way, and we all made a dash to the scooters and the Bubble. I managed to get away for about a mile before I was pulled over by a police patrol car, the officer walked over to the Bubble and was peering in through the Sun Roof, and said: "Alright lads, we've a report of a disturbance up the road between a group of mods and skinheads, a lot of trouble, and furthermore, we have a report that these mods had a Bubble car which was red, and had a black line down the middle... just like yours, was this you?"

I thought about my reply carefully, I said: "No, that

was not us! There are a good few Bubbles like this one in Bristol. The policeman smiled: "OK lads I suggest you leave the area pronto." I took his advice and left, it was a close call.

On another occasion, I parked the Bubble outside my house which was on a hill. About an hour later my neighbor knocked on the door and said:

"Jon, you might want to know that your Bubble car is sat in the middle of the Gloucester Road and everybody is having to go around it."

There it was, bang in the middle of the road, about 250 feet away, with about 50 people looking and laughing. I must have left the hand brake off and the Bubble had set off unmanned down the hill, avoiding several parked cars and came to rest in the middle of the very busy Gloucester Road. I set off on my walk of shame to retrieve my Bubble and was met with more loud laughter as I sheepishly climbed aboard. I made an easy decision, sell it. I got £175, what a huge mistake that was, as they are now worth many thousands.

A few memorable one liners I used to get about the Bubble:

"I am not getting in THAT."

"So this is a BMW, is it really?"

"Jon, where have you parked your cricket ball?"

"I suppose somebody has got to own it."

"I like your BMW key ring, but that's as far as it goes."

"Jon, where is your tricycle?"

Enough about the transportation of the day, and

more about the fashion... I particularly liked paisley cravats and had about four quality pieces, I also liked boating blazers and Seersucker jackets. I had around 10 such jackets, some I bought in second-hand shops, some in those quirky USA second-hand clothes shops in London, and a few I had hand-made. I particularly had a craving for a Union Jack jacket like Pete Townshend's. I did not want to buy a copy jacket from Carnaby Street because they looked cheap and terrible, like they were made from a printed tea towel, I wanted a real one!.

After a late night drinking in town, I was walking home with a group of friends and I caught a glimpse of a Union Jack flying high on top of one of the department stores. I walked over to the base of the building and noticed that the corner brickwork of the building was staggered, in fact you could climb up. Egged on by my friends, I started to scale the corner of the building, it took what seemed forever to reach the top. I released the flag from its mast and wrapped it a good few times around my waist and clambered back down to a round of applause. I kept the flag wrapped around my waist until I reached home. Once home, I unfurled the flag which, to my astonishment was massive, truly massive. It was 12 feet long by around 8 feet tall, it was way too big to turn into a jacket, and I still have that flag to this day. It looked very small flying above the department store, in fact I had climbed more than 100 feet to reach it. Stupid boy!

A little while later I managed to purchase a good-quality original canvas Union Jack that was of a jacket-capable size. I set off on my scooter for a tour of local tailors with the flag in a bag. I tried many tailors, most said it was impossible, but I suspect they were just not interested. I finally ended up in a very small tailors shop that was close to Fred Baker's Cycle Shop on Stokes Croft. I was met by a middle-aged, very short and rotund Nigerian gentleman tailor, and he was a real gent too. He spent an hour or so explaining the complexity of the pattern, and how it needed to be symmetrical in design to have any meaning. He really knew his stuff, he said, one mistake on the cutting the pattern from the flag and it was all over. We agreed on £100 for the jacket, which included a bright blue silk lining and matching red and blue covered buttons (made from the flag), it would take around one month to complete. One hundred pounds was around two week's wages back then. I stopped by every week to catch up and watch the jacket's progress, I believe it was an extremely difficult job, and I am absolutely sure that this tailor spent much more time on the jacket than he anticipated. Finally the jacket was ready and it was absolutely perfect, a quality replica of Mr Townshend's jacket that was probably equal, if not better. The symmetry of the stripes on the sleeves was perfect on mine, whereas Mr Townshend's… Ahem! I only wore the jacket on stage with Mayfair.

  I had several stage suits for the band, and I never altered the configuration of these stage suits. With the Union Jack jacket I would wear a plain white shirt with 1-inch white knitted tie, white slack trousers and white leather Chelsea boots with a black gusset. Proper stuff that looked great on stage.

The local mods who got a good look at the Union Jacket immediately commissioned the Nigerian tailor to make complete suits for them. He had a steady stream of business from the mods, and he deserved it.

Onto the footwear... for me there was only four types of acceptable mod footwear:
1. Original Clarke's desert boots.
2. Bowling shoes (as bright and as decorative as you could buy).
3. Chelsea boots.
4. Suede brogues.

Moccasins, tassle Loafers and bloody white socks were definitely not acceptable mod footwear, but were always worn by the German parka-clad mod wannabes. I include the loafer as non-mod because most loafers worn during the late 1970s mod revival were the skinhead type tassle loafer, and not the plain penny loafer occasionally worn by mods of the 60s.

The correct attire to be worn under the suit, jacket or parka was a plain or patterned quality shirt worn with 1-inch silk or knitted tie or a plain polo shirt or roll-top sweaters or knitted sweater. Trousers should be good quality (ideally tailored) plain or patterned slacks.

In both mod communities I was getting a reputation for being a bit (or a lot) of a mod preacher. I was so deeply devoted to the 1960s roots of mod that I often frowned upon many of the 1970s revivalist mods, but I did not care. I was at the peak of my very own creation, I was the lead singer in one of Bristol's very few mod bands, I was the chairman of the Westside Unicorns Scooter Club, and I was a 'face' to a lot of people. I felt I had a duty to uphold the good ethics of mod, I felt mod had chosen me as its crusader, and I was not going to let mod down.

One thing, I honestly believe is that the mods of the 1960s had a much easier time of it the first time round, they were the masses, and the only sworn enemy of any number were rockers, but in truth, and statistically, the trouble-maker rockers were small in numbers. In the 1970s Mod revival a minority mod movement had to face massed tribes of skins, punks and bikers and just about anybody else of a similar age.

I have never had a skinhead as a friend. I never would, I still hate them the most, even now. They were very disruptive and because they had little to do within the 'skin thing' when it suited them, they joined in with mod events that more often than not ended in violence that they caused. I can never forgive that, and most of the trouble that I got involved in was with skinheads.

I booked a coach for Bristol mods to attend a mod event in Swindon. We needed to quickly pull into the services on the way to pick up a mod who was finishing work in the services restaurant. I was the only person to get off the coach, and as I walked into the services alone, a group of three skinheads confronted me. They abused and harassed me but could not cause too much trouble inside the services. I collected the chap who was joining us, and returned to the coach. I explained what had happened and the coach erupted and emptied into the services. As more than 40 of us charged through the front door the look on faces on those three skins, who were by now playing the pinball machine, was priceless. The Unicorn's had a fair amount of mad ones and the skinheads were soon left wishing they had kept quiet.

The skins of the late 70s used the early skin reputation for violence as a fear factor, yet, they often barked much more than they could actually bite, it was usually a bluff.

Bored one day, three of us decided on a weekday trip to Weston-super-Mare for a few beers. Weston had a fair number of skins, and we knew it was a risk, so we did not take our scooters, we drove down by car, but we were tooled up, just in case.

We'd only been there about an hour, when we were confronted by a small group of skins outside one of the amusement parlours, which was par for the course. I quickly produced a hammer from inside my parka and waved it in front of them. The skins looked totally shocked and they immediately withdrew to the inside of the amusements and disappeared out of sight. We saw them again several times during the day, and they just looked the other way. It was a great day out that saw us banned from two pubs on the return journey to Bristol. The second pub banned my friend for re-enacting our confrontation with the skins, but instead of using a hammer, he took a lighted log from the pub fire, waving it lit and smoking above his head cursing, or was it me that did that?

A skinhead lived a few streets away from me. He had been a skin for a long time, from around 1975. He was a few years younger than me, quite tall and had a very round head, so much so, that in my local mod circle he was known as 'Goldfish Bowl Head. We had always somehow managed to avoid each other but there was bad blood between us as I quite often spoke of him in a derogatory manner in front of locals, and he did likewise about me. The comments we both made filtered back to the both of us, it was inevitable that one day our paths would cross and they did.

It was 10pm, about seven scooters and around 10 of us were parked outside Shwartz Bros burger bar on the Gloucester Road, we were minding our own business, chatting, eating our burgers. Suddenly four cars screeched to a halt directly in front of us, about 20 lads jumped out of the cars. They were from the White Lion pub further up the road, they had a report that a group of mods were down the road and decided to come down mob-handed to make sure our evening ended badly, and so it did.

Surprise was the key, they were out of the cars and upon us in an instant, they had wooden bats, clubs, all kinds of horrible weapons. I took a very strong blow to the back of my head and fell from my scooter to the pavement, I curled up into a ball as best as I could to protect myself as four of them went to town on me, I passed out, cannot remember how long, but when I came to I saw Goldfish Bowl Head being led away in handcuffs, I was shouting all kinds of profanity at him vowing my vengeance upon him, he was not smiling any more, nor could he look me in the eye, finally our paths crossed.

I had three cracked ribs, a cut hand, broken finger, black eye, I was lucky, several of our group needed overnight hospitalisation, all this happened within sight of my home, it was the one and only time that I took a beating through being mod.

I never saw Goldfish Bowl Head again, and later heard that he was spending time at her majesty's leisure.

Steamers Night Club, had become the town's main club for the mods to congregate, it was a club on three levels: small downstairs bar area, the middle was a dance floor, and the top floor was another bar. On Thursdays and Saturdays it belonged to the mods and anybody else who fancied visiting, needless to say, it saw much violence.

I can recall on one summer's evening, with all the scooters lined up in the central reservation outside of Steamers. Four budding rockabillies were driving up and down in a large American car hurling abuse at the mods lined up outside. They decided to knock over several of the scooters before driving off at high speed.

This was stupid, a big flash American car is pretty recognisable. A few moments later a mod reported that he knew who owned this car and where it is parked… a plan is hatched.

Around 11pm, several weeks later, three mods parked up in a car, further down the road, was the American car. The mod car set off down the street with its lights off, gathering speed as it hurtled towards the American car. I have been told that the mods were humming the Dambusters anthem as they sped along. As they neared the front of the American car, they shouted 'bombs away' and threw two breeze blocks into the American car windscreen. The mods disappeared into the night.

This was winter, and a week later a report reached Steamers of the rockabillies being spotted driving without a front windscreen and looking absolutely frozen in the car.

The visit of Avonmouth Rugby Club to Steamers one Sunday night is also memorable. The fighting took place on all three levels of the club, I and two friends defended the staircase that led from the street to the middle dance floor. I could hear fighting going on in the downstairs bar and also upstairs. Many friends were injured, it was like a battlefield. I had chosen my drinking companions very well that night, the two sturdy have-a-go mods alongside me never backed down. We were all trapped inside, it was fight and get hit, or just get hit. Luckily we came out of it relatively unharmed, mainly through our choice to defend the staircase, those in the downstairs bar suffered the worst of the attack, it was not pretty.

These were truly very violent times, I cannot emphasise this enough. A few of the mods, like me, grew up on Bristol's football terraces during the early to late 70s, the most notorious decade for football violence. I firmly believe that if you were around and in the thick of the violence back then, you already knew how to handle yourself, and how to react within a crowd intent on violence. The violence that mods were involved in was similar to football violence because it usually involved groups of people. In fact, I can only remember two skirmishes that were one-on-one, and both of them were mod-on-mod.

The flip side to the violence, and what made things special about being a mod, was the friendship that we shared as mods whatever part of the country we were from.

I committed myself to mod from 1979 until 1984, by this time I was married with two young daughters. I was 24 and life was changing. I watched on as mods began adopting rockabilly or scooter boy fashion. This was not for me and as 1984 slipped away, I did too.

PUNKS ON SCOOTERS

Jerry Cripps, Steamers DJ

My journey to becoming a DJ at Steamers started with Friday night outings to Romeo & Juliet's night club in Nelson Street in 1980. I'm from Keynsham and a lot of my friends (other than Sean Beech) didn't see the attraction of clubbing in Bristol, but I loved the escape of losing yourself on the dance floor to loud music.

One Friday night my rubbish attempts at chatting up girls were actually successful. This led to a relationship with Sue Hall.

This relationship, enjoyable as it was, was not the defining moment that led me to Steamers. This happened when Sue's dad, Dave Hall, decided to jointly purchase a run-down night club in Prince Street opposite Jury's Hotel. This would be a great place for him and his Avonmouth Rugby Club friends to party. That night club was to become Steamers.

Being rather handy, I was invited to get involved in refitting the club which I was more than happy to do because what I really wanted was to get my hands on the DJ equipment.

Dave's idea was to have an over 25s night with a Sixties DJ on Thursdays. My only knowledge of Sixties music involved the usual suspects such as Little Eva's 'Locomotion', 'Twist and Shout' by The Beatles and 'Let's Twist' Again by Chubby Checker. So Dave decided to bring in a specialist Sixties DJ and I covered Friday, Saturday and Sunday playing chart, jazz funk and also reggae.

APPENDICES

The local scooter clubs heard about the Sixties night and descended in great numbers. Dave was happy to oblige this unexpected crowd, but they wanted a different sort of Sixties music to the sounds on offer. So Dave approached me to see if I would take over the Thursdays as well. My knowledge of soul music and what mods and scooter boys were interested in was zero. But I was happy to give it a go and I was enjoying my new-found fame of being a DJ.

Dave provided me with a few soul albums and I got together some tunes from recommendations from the crowd that was now also taking over the other nights over the weekend. So I was given lists of favourite tunes and people brought down their own records to boost my limited collection. Although most of the records made their way back to their owners I am still in possession of two albums of Mod Classics so if the rightful owner wants these back they can contact me.

As the weeks went by I started to understand mod music and began scouring second-hand record shops to find that gem that someone had told me to look out for; you can still find me flipping through old vinyl with that hope of finding that next monster floor filler that will make me smile when I play it out.

Two people from Steamers stand out in my memory Andrew Harvey known as RV and Jock, I never did find out his real name. These two were the bridge from me to everyone else in the crowd. They knew everyone and if they didn't they soon did.

PUNKS ON SCOOTERS

They brought me (a dweeby out-of-town boy with a very Christian upbringing) into the dark and dirty world of the Bristol scooter scene. This was exciting and I can remember many times, being the only one with a car, having to drive them to a pub to meet one of their mates who had just been released from prison and was blowing the cash he'd been given on release. Also, being the Steamers DJ meant that the girls thought I was cool – a whole new world.

This world was very different to what I was used to. On a Sunday I still went to church to satisfy my parents and then I'd go to Steamers to DJ and revel in the not so Christian activities. Drinking and then fighting seemed to be a normal activity at Steamers.

The mix of people certainly made the atmosphere tense but that was what was exciting about Steamers. Putting mods, skinheads, rugby players, soul boys and black guys in one place was never going to be easy. Feeling a sense of responsibility, initially I would wade in to help break up the fights that seemed to happen every night and I became very good at a full nelson. As time passed the fighting seemed to be so normal I just carried on regardless with the exception of a couple of rucks that stick in my memory.

One night a particularly large fight took over the whole of the dance floor and I was keeping what distance I could by hiding in the DJ booth. For those who were not fortunate enough to visit Steamers, the DJ booth had vertical bars in front of the decks and looked a bit like a jail except the bars were to keep people out rather than in. I felt safe until I leaned slightly forward. Someone leaned in through the bars grabbed my hair (I did have some then) pulled my head through the bars and started punching me in the face. I eventually got free by leaving some of my hair behind in his hand.

My other memory is of a similarly large fight, I was staying in the DJ booth now with the experience to stay away from the bars. Suddenly I felt a pull on my arm from someone who came to the side entrance to the booth. He was gesturing to something in his hand and I eventually realised he wanted me to have whatever it was. It was a knife with what looked like blood on it. Shocked I quickly discarded it under the decks with no idea what to do next, so did nothing and waited for the scrap to disperse. It turned out that someone did get stabbed but I never did find out what happened to the knife as when I went to recover it, it was gone.

Despite the fighting I have many happy memories of Steamers. The spectacle of the scooters lined up on the central reservation outside the club was fantastic. The pride and work that went into these was incredible. I remember one guy being very popular as he worked in a plating factory so could get parts chromed on the sly. The dancing and the skinhead who walked around on his hands with his arms tucked underneath his legs pretending to be a spider; drinking the slops from the drip tray to save money; carrying RV home because he'd passed out; Dave cooking me the hottest chilli he could make at the end of the night and watching people's faces as they tried to steal some...

  As with all great things it came to an end. I try not to hold on to bad memories so that is probably why I do not have any recollection of it actually ending. People just seemed to drift apart but that time will always be with me for ever and the music still lives on. Keep The Faith.

APPENDICES

The Newbeats and Colonel Kilgore's Vietnamese Formation Surf Team by **Michael W Salter**

Andy Baker was the epitome of a mod. Tall fresh-faced and always smartly dressed. From a distance he had a passing resemblance to a very young Paul McCartney. Unlike me, he was quite happy to wear his love for The Beatles if not on his sleeve then certainly on the bodywork of his Vespa. Andy had meticulously searched through his huge collection of 60s paraphernalia and cut out his favourite photos of those four loveable lads from Liverpool, which he then painstakingly stuck all over his scooter. If Andy was making a statement then it was surely that he was a huge Beatles fan and unlike me he didn't care who knew.

Not only did Andy have a passing resemblance to everybody's favourite mop tops but he also had a great ability for playing the electric guitar, writing catchy songs and carrying a tune. In no uncertain terms, Andy had a gift for music.

Little did I know when I first met him that Andy had also been harbouring his own secret plan to achieve musical world domination just like his Merseyside heroes, a plan that was to go on to be known as The Severn Sound.

All Andy needed was a few fellow Bristolians who shared his vision and an unshakeable faith in his road map to success... I had the requisite mop of brown hair so I duly stepped up to the plate.

Having struggled for years to master various

musical instruments especially my six-string guitar, we decided the odds would be more in our favour if they were reduced by 33 per cent, and so after very little deliberation I became the bass player.

I'm still not sure where the band's name came from, but very soon we were no longer mere mortals, we were The Newbeats. We played self-penned songs that we truly believed would one day change the world.

Move over John, Paul, George and that other one, The Newbeats were hot on your shiny cuban heels. All we needed was a good demo tape and fame and fortune would surely be ours.

After months of assiduous practising we booked ourselves into the newly established Chipping Sodbury Fame Recording Studios owned by a rather fatherly Ray Markham. Ray had a very impressive résumé that included once working with the Nolan Sisters and yes believe it or not, that was more than impressive enough for us to be convinced that Ray Markham was our man.

That day in the studio was a wonderful experience, especially hearing songs that you had laboured over and practised come to life when played back over the reassuringly expensive sound system. For a moment it was like listening to some wonderful outtakes off the *Hard Days Night* album. With the Rickenbacker guitar jangling over each beautifully crafted tune, my plodding bass lines and Andy's west country voice belting out such self-penned songs as 'How Can I Tell?', and 'She Loves You' it really did sound like the stars in heaven were truly aligned, all was going to plan.

Sitting there entranced by the mixing desk play back, I had but one thought on my mind... Fuck The Beatles, here come The Newbeats!

It wasn't long before the ever-hungry local press picked up the story with the slightly misspelt headline 'If The Newbetas move quickly they could be big'. Buoyed with a somewhat unflattering photo but favourable review I did what I thought was best for the band's future... I left.

There was no, '"Wait, wait come back' moment or even a gold watch. It was obviously preordained, at least in Andy's mind, that The Newbeats' original bass player should fall by the wayside, just like the one in The Beatles. I was always convinced that Andy felt I had let the band down somewhat by not dropping down dead, just like Stuart Sutcliffe (The Beatles' original bass player) had done all those years previously.

I'm glad to say that even with me still alive the band went from strength to strength, recruiting new members, and building a small but loyal following around the pubs and clubs of Bristol.

Sadly things went very quickly downhill when the very much hyped Newbeats were unceremoniously swept aside by a virtually unknown band called Blue Riverside who gave a stunning performance at a well-attended battle of the bands competition.

With the dream of Severn Sound musical world domination in tatters, Andy left for pastures new, and without its driving force leading the way, the band very quickly disintegrated.

The world, or even Bristol it would seem, was not ready for 'Newbeatsmania'.

Unlike The Newbeats, Colonel Kilgore's Vietnamese Formation Surf Team were for a while the most popular band in Bristol. Inspired by the film *Apocalypse Now*, the Kilgore's adopted scooter boy and girl fashion and shared the ethos of scooters, music and alcohol.

Scooterists readily identified with The Kilgore's stage dress – military boots, combat trousers, green T-shirts and dog tags. Each band member had their own carefully chosen stage name to suit their persona. There was Chuck on electric six-string guitar, Chuck on drums, Chuck on electric bass guitar, and on vocals just in case it was all getting a little confusing, yes you've guessed it… Chuck. The three female backing singers were unsurprisingly called The Chuckettes. To complete the show, The Kilgore's had their own Military Police-style security with authentic long wooden truncheons.

Unlike the mod type bands that were still doing the rounds, The Kilgore's were fun and offered something creative and new. Every gig was a major event. The day of the show The Kilgore G.I.s crammed into a U.S Army vehicle and drove round the town announcing their show (or mission, as they called it) with the help of a megaphone.

The excitement levels before each performance were always through the roof, aided by the cleverly orchestrated build up. The stage set included imitation palm trees, surf boards and torn battle-weary Stars and Stripes flags. On occasions Sean Parry aka Dr Napalm would read his poetry from the book Dr Napalm's Bumper Book For Boys which would set the scene before the lights dimmed and ushered in the sound of approaching U.S helicopter gunships, which seemed to be literally hovering over our heads.

With the room in almost total darkness, search lights from above weaved over and amongst the expectant crowd. People looked skyward just to check there really wasn't a helicopter coming in to land. It felt that real. The whole experience was heightened with the faint but rising sound of Wagner's 'Ride of the Valkyries' underscoring the hypnotic sound of helicopter rotor blades slicing through the cigarette smoke-thickened air. It really was an assault on the senses, and as near as any of us would get to being entertained like some US Marines at a USO show along the Nung River.

The band's entrance was announced by spectacular explosions adding to the smoke-filled room. Having built such a tense atmosphere, The Kilgore's would lurch into such self-penned songs as 'Surfin' offa' Saigon', 'Napalm Blues', 'Sputnik Rock' and my favourite 'Paradise Cowboy'. With the superbly choreographed build-up having done its job, the band were guaranteed many encores.

Although not musically the best band on the circuit, they were the most visually pleasing and charismatic band that Bristol has ever produced.

Their final performance was at a sold-out at Goldiggers night club in Chippenham. The Kilgore's weren't just a band, they were a military assault on the senses.

ALSO AVAILABLE THE SOUNDTRACK TO THE ERA
MODS, POWER POP, SCOOTER BOYS 1979-1987
VISIT BRISTOLARCHIVERECORDS.COM

NEXT INSTALMENT COMING SOON...

Now they turn their attention to another SUB CULTURE...

BRISTOL BOYS MAKE MORE NOISE!
MODS, POWER POP, SCOOTER BOYS 1979-1987

Feat: Mayfair, Thin Air, The Rimshots, The A.T's, Huw Gower (The Records) The Gross Club, Cass Carnaby Five, The Review and more.

OUT NOW
CD & Digital Download

Preorder now from: www.bristolarchiverecords.com | www.amazon.co.uk | iTunes

Distributed by Shellshock / SRD ARC287CD www.bristolarchiverecords.com BRISTOL ARCHIVE RECORDS